To Maria and Brent

© 1994 Page One Publishing Pte Ltd
Block 4 Pasir Panjang Road
#08-33 Alexandra Distripark
Singapore 0511

Distributed worldwide (excluding South East Asia) by
Könemann Verlagsgesellschaft mbH
Bonner Str. 126, D-50968 Köln

Designed by Duet Design Pte Ltd
Colour Separation by Colour Scan Pte Ltd
Typecasting by Superskill Graphics Pte Ltd
Printed and bound by Tien Wah Press, Singapore

Printed in Singapore
ISBN 981-00-4032-6

*Right: A close-up view of an elegant Thai
manuscript cabinet.*
Overleaf: Amandari Resort, Bali.

Tropical Architecture and Interiors

TRADITION-BASED DESIGN OF INDONESIA · MALAYSIA · SINGAPORE · THAILAND

TEXT AND PHOTOGRAPHY

TAN HOCK BENG

PAGE ONE PUBLISHING PTE LTD

"Of all things, I honour beginnings.

I believe, though, that what was has always

been, and what is has always been, and

what will be has always been."

- Louis Kahn

Dining pavilion in one of Amanpuri's private villas.

Contents

"Poetry is what really lets us dwell. But through what do we attain to a dwelling place? Through building. Poetic creation, which lets us dwell, is a kind of building."

- Martin Heidegger

I treasure my time as a practitioner of architecture. At the same time, I spent many richly savoured hours exploring other interests within this wonderful discipline that at its best, provide the most sublime stage-sets for human drama. Among them is architectural photography, a field explored by many serious photographers for its multi-dimensional formal qualities. I believe a truly successful photographic documentation can only be made when the photographer is genuinely interested in the architecture and fully appreciate the designer's intentions.

However, the photographic medium is unable to capture spatial quality and time because space is always experienced as a totality. Egyptian architect Hassan Fathy once defined architecture as "the space between the walls and not the walls". The photographic image can only capture the walls.

Ezra Stoller, a great contemporary master of architectural photography, says, "It is architecture which is of primary interest to me, with photography being simply the medium for communicating its idea." It is the architecture of Southeast Asia with its manifold possibilities which is of fundamental interest to me, especially the poetics of built form. Examples abound of buildings which involve our whole range of sensory perception. Their tectonic presence constitute a reverberating tropical reverie.

The idea for this book was generated as a result of the numerous slides that I exposed during my trips around this vast region. There is such an incredibly rich reservoir of images, sounds and smells. Bali, especially, has remained vividly in my mind as one of the most fascinating places I have ever been.

I was also indirectly inspired by the exquisite prints of John Thompson. One of the great figures of 19th century photography, Thompson was famous for his hauntingly captivating images of the Far East. His lenses captured scenes of daily life and architecture with such a vivid sense of immediacy that was both exquisite and powerful.

The contents of this volume provide an occasion to take a broad view. This is only a limited selection, intended primarily as illustrations and as visual statements. The intention here is to sample architecture in Southeast Asia not as a comprehensive guide, but selectively, so that a sufficient range of buildings which evoke the unique aura of the tropics – buildings which are tangible witnesses to their place and time – blending primordial and poetic presence, can be presented. It is hoped that they should act as catalysts in the process of the reader's discovery of the sensitive physicality of the architecture. In the words of Susan Sontag: "Photographs, which cannot by themselves explain anything, are inexhaustible invitations to deduction, speculation, and fantasy."

I am neither advocating a nostalgic return to the forms of the past by encouraging the mere ransacking of history nor promoting pastiches of cultural stereotypes. The intention has also not been to delve into lengthy debates on the critical aspects of an authentic expression which hope to achieve a convincing synthesis of the old and new. Instead, the purpose is to showcase traditional architecture as well as tradition-based contemporary design that either re-invigorate or reinterpret the vernacular, and at the same time, exhibit hypersensitised readings of the hot and humid surroundings.

The German uses an appropriate term – "stimmung" – to describe the "character" or "mood" of a particular place. It is something intangible that can only be manifested by an appropriate architecture. The poetics of Southeast Asian built form that manifest this "stimmung" is something I hope to capture. To me the tropics is not so much a region as it is a feeling; a feeling that must be understood intuitively. The book can best be defined as an attempt to distill the essence of this feeling.

This is done by categorising architectural elements into some broad and conventional classifications. They are by no means a scholarly taxonomy; rather, a random grouping of irreducible elements of architecture in the tropics in order to give an impression of the intrinsic qualities peculiar to Southeast Asian buildings. However, they are not static entities. They should be viewed within a hierarchy of relationships that contributes to the creation of built forms.

Photographing these buildings in the attempt to capture their breathtaking verve has been an arduous but deeply satisfying endeavour. I fully agree with critic Paul Goldberger's observation that "the photographer's responsibility is to give the building the fairest chance to speak for itself." I hope that this book passes on some of the profound enjoyment that I have derived from the architecture of this region. The best of these wonderfully crafted buildings are capable of eliciting strong emotions. Like the exquisite artefacts of Southeast Asia, they possess the virtues of craft: function, beauty, harmony and poetry.

Tan Hock Beng
Singapore 1993

*T*here is not and never has been a singular, definitive tropical architectural style. Countries in the tropics, which comprise a wide belt around the middle of the earth do not, of course, share a univalent cultural or social framework. Sandwiched between the Pacific and Indian oceans, the Southeast Asian region has from the earliest recorded history developed its own identity through the practice of animism as well as continued contact with other cultures.

An immensely varied region, Southeast Asia is a term that gained common usage only after World War II. It describes in a broad geographical sense, the territories of the Indo-Chinese Peninsula, the Philippines and the vast archipelago of Indonesia. The insular region also includes Brunei, Malaysia and Singapore. Together they form one of the most diverse and culturally richest areas of the world. This populous region, consisting of more than 300 million people, also has a rich diversity of architecture shaped by a succession of foreign influences over a long period of time.

Between 600 and 400 BC, the Dong Son culture, also known as the Metal Age, passed from China to Vietnam and subsequently the rest of Southeast Asia. Archaeologists have discovered magnificent bronze drums as well as other art motifs belonging to this era on the remote islands of Indonesia, leading to the theory that Dong Son migrants had an early impact on the indigenous culture of island Southeast Asia. One of the largest prehistoric artefacts ever discovered in the region – the "Moon of Pejeng", a bronze kettledrum – is probably from Dong Son and is now kept in a village temple in Gianyar, Bali.

These drums have elaborate surface decorations depicting houses raised on stilts, boats and human activities. Other archaeological finds gave further indications of Chinese contact as far back as the Han dynasty, while the 6th century BC Indian epic, the "Ramayana" as well as the "Mahabharata" provided ample evidence of early Indian contact. Their Sanskrit texts were translated by the inhabitants of the Indonesian archipelago and have since inspired numerous dramas, dances and architectural decorations.

"The past should be altered by the present as much as the present is directed by the past... the difference between the present and the past is that the conscious present is an awareness of the past in a way and to an extent which the past's awareness of itself cannot show."

- T. S. Eliot

Chinese and Indian penetrations into Southeast Asia were prompted not by military expansion, but by trade. Drawn by the abundance of gold, tin, teak and spices, these sea-faring traders established trading colonies and brought with them their languages, religions, political concepts and architectural principles. Some of the greatest achievements of Asian architecture are the magnificent Angkor Wat in Khmer, the massive Hindu temple complex at Prambanan (also known as Loro Jonggrang) and the noble Buddhist stupa of Borobudur in Central Java.

Angkor Wat, a Hindu shrine dedicated to the god Vishnu, was built in the early 12th century. Abandoned for about five centuries, it is a masterpiece of order and balance. Another colossal Hindu shrine is the Loro Jonggrang complex built at the end of the 10th century and considered to be Java's most elegantly proportioned Hindu temple. Borobudur, the world's largest Buddhist monument, is certainly one of the most impressive structures ever created by man. These mega-structures bear witness to the powerful foreign influences.

Hinduism and Buddhism were the dominant religions in many parts of Southeast Asia and flourished as patrons of art and architecture. The use of masonry in the architecture of the region was directly linked to the propagation of these faiths originating from India. Buddhism reigned supreme especially in Myanmar (Burma), Cambodia and Thailand. Two movements later developed within Buddhism to form Theravada and Mahayana.

The Sumatran kingdom of Srivijaya became the centre for the study of Mahayana Buddhism during the 7th century. This movement inspired the construction of impressive stone mandalas that symbolised the ordered cosmos. In the mid-9th century, the Hindu kingdom of Mataram, the paramount kingdom of Central Java that was strongly influenced by India, made an especially lasting impression on Javanese architecture. The religious component introduced a complex set of symbolic allusions into the architec-

Detail from a Thai mural painting, depicting the walled compounds of a Buddhist monastery.

Scene of a 'floating market' in Bangkok. There are 3,000,000 km of such inland waterways in the rural hinterland of Thailand.

ture of Southeast Asia. This phenomenon is further complicated by divergent religious trends and syncretic hybrids of great vitality. Such variations were reflected to some extent in architecture.

Nevertheless, scholars now recognise that Indian and Chinese influences have been greatly over-emphasised. Southeast Asia is not a mere cultural appendage of India or China, though its art and architecture have their roots principally in the Hindu-Buddhist cosmological model due to its proximity to these two established civilisations. It has not simply been a passive receptacle of cultural forces from these countries. The basic underlying similarities present throughout Southeast Asian societies have been undeservedly neglected by many academicians.

Although many monuments were based on the traditions of the Indian architectural manuals, "Shilapashastras", the history of the region's architecture also witnessed the evolution of autonomous styles which owed much to local traditions of bamboo and timber construction and other local impulses.

Archaeological evidence shows that the earliest stone and brick buildings were apparently modelled after the forms of timber architecture and that Southeast Asia has had its own distinct forms of expression since Neolithic times. The native artistic traditions also had an Austronesian heritage dating back several millennia, which were fairly advanced and unrivalled anywhere in India or China.

As historian Daniel Hall points out, "...after the introduction of Hinduism and Buddhism, the religious ideas and practices of earlier times persisted with immense vitality, and in coming to terms with them, both religions were profoundly changed." Thus beneath the common foundations, we can discern an inextricable intermingling of ideas and an extensive interplay of mutual influence.

Within this general framework, there are naturally varying social phenomena and economic climates, and a rich diversity of art forms. Many have further fragmented sub-cultures, all co-existing in an easy pluralism. Indonesia, for example, has more than 350 separate ethnic groups, many with distinct languages, social systems and religions spread over its 13,600 islands. It is thus misleading to talk of a national expression in building or even a monolithic regionalism in these multifaceted and syncretisitic societies of Southeast Asia.

Architecturally, there are many shared characteristics which are highly suggestive of a similar origin. However, the only real unifier is the primary concern with a singly immutable factor – the uniformly hot and wet climate. Tropical conditions can be energy-sapping. Greek philosophers even called the tropical areas the "torrid zone", or "the hot lands", believing the region to be uninhabitable because it was "too hot". Early Western sojourners found the debilitating tropic heat particularly unwholesome. In the 18th century, Batavia (Dutch name for Jakarta throughout 350 years of colonial rule) was perceived as the Westerner's graveyard in Southeast Asia.

The region is also generally known as "Asia of the Monsoons" because of the prevailing monsoon weather that affects nearly all Southeast Asia. Topography creates some climatic irregularities like typhoons and tropical cyclones but generally, the climate is characterised by intense sunshine, heavy rainfall, prevailing winds, high humidity and equable temperatures. Evaporative cooling is greatly reduced due to the high humidity, which averages about 75 per cent or more. Temperatures average between 22°C and 32°C, with only minor seasonal variation. Climate is clearly one of the prime factors of culture, and therefore built form. It is also the mainspring for all the sensual qualities that add up to a vital tropical architecture.

The tropical house type can be seen in the broad verandahs, the fluid interaction between inside and outside, cool courtyards, steeply pitched roofs with wide eaves and

In Southeast Asia, the local subsistence economy has always been based on wet rice cultivation.

A Balinese priest in a prayer session. There is an inextricable intermingling of influences in the religious beliefs and architecture of Southeast Asia.

deep overhangs, concern for shade and cross-ventilation, and the prevalent use of timber. The use of timber as a building material is sensible since it is abundant, locally available and has a low thermal mass so that minimal heat is transmitted into the building. Bamboo is also commonly employed for construction because it is widely available and easily replenished. Its drawbacks are its short life span and a large variability in moisture content.

Light-weight, semi-permeable walls have always been a feature of buildings in this part of the world. Their role is to maximise the interface between the inside space and the surroundings. Instead of excluding the weather and isolating a building's occupants from the external environment, the architecture filters the outside selectively through a system of louvred openings. The buildings thus offer immediate and direct contact with the lush landscape. Open lattice screens reinforce the physics of feeling comfortable. High ceilings also encourage the free flow of air through the building. All these delightful qualities are triggers to the local collective memory.

Besides their religious symbolism, the lavish stone bas-reliefs at Angkor depict pointed gable wooden houses with floors raised high on stilts, demonstrating the ancient origins of this particular dwelling type. Research has shown that the whole of Southeast Asia was historically covered by wooden houses raised some two metres off the ground, with the exception of coastal Vietnam, the eastern parts of Java, Bali and West Lombok. The absence of a stilt-building tradition in these areas deserves some speculative interpretation. This is generally attributed to Indian influence in Bali and Lombok.

Dwellings raised on stilts protect the occupants from floods, provide under-floor ventilation and a semi-protected space underneath for storage as well as keeping of domestic animals. Built of local materials, such as teak or bamboo, these houses with steeply pitched roofs were the efforts of local craftsmen and artisans.

Many of the architects working in the region today appear to have forgotten how to design bearing in mind the climate and landscape. They are now caught in the homogenising forces of the mass media and are repeating the built mediocrities of international fashion. Each commission is seen as a vehicle for egoistic self-expression while little importance is attached to memory and continuity.

These glitz-and-tinsel architectural fads and stylistic masquerades have resulted in similar-looking buildings to be erected from the tropics to the arctics. Such trendy aestheticism finds indiscriminate patronage in many rapidly developing cities. This is especially evident in Bangkok, where wholesale imitations of Western neo-classical styles are used in a rampant and often bizarre manner.

On the other hand, the finest works of some architects reject such imported trivialities and facile eclecticism. They are also turning away from the barren functionalism of the dull International Style which seeks to impose a homogeneity that does not take into account local realities. These architects' awareness of working in a specific spatial and temporal environment is strong and confident. They are producing an architectural ensemble that is environmentally tuned, with a sensual refinement and sure sense of place. It directly touches the imagination through the senses: visual, tactile, auditory as well as olfactory. Inspiration is drawn from a reverence for the land in the advent of an architecture that has a genuine affinity to the context – an architecture of 'place'.

In this collection, we celebrate this special lifestyle, where the mood is at once tranquil and festive, and where the possibilities offered by the varied elements of the enchanting surroundings have been exploited with clear-sightedness. The buildings' vitality derives from a poise between tradition and innovation, while the aesthetics refers to the attributes of materials and techniques. Above all, they are eloquent with the spirit of the place and congenial to the aspirations and values of these traditional cultures. A cursory view offers endless delights.

Intricate costumes and elegant gestures of young Balinese girls. In this collection, we celebrate this special lifestyle, where the mood is at once tranquil and festive.

The distinctive roof forms of traditional Thai dwellings.

Imagery

"The true basis for the more serious

study of the art of architecture lies

with those more humble indigenous

buildings everywhere... Functions

are truthfully conceived and

rendered invariably with natural

feeling. Results are often beautiful

and always instinctive."

- Frank Lloyd Wright

The increasing use of traditional forms as a source of contemporary design has been widely discussed in recent years, gaining momentum particularly in Third World nations. In the face of a self-indulgent architecture of Postmodernism and the reductive universality of Modern architecture, these rapidly developing countries have begun to look at built form as an expression of their own aspirations and identities. Furthermore, within the vast variety of multi-faceted traditions are the repositories of history and an intricate fabric of myths and symbols which can be tapped creatively.

In the post-colonial era, when developing nations rushed to embrace global homogeneity and Western technology, efforts to preserve local traditions were largely ignored. The empty banalities of allegedly progressive forms were thoughtlessly and indiscriminately borrowed by practitioners. Rural traditions were commonly despised and readily seen as "countrified" symbols of anachronism.

But today, the ideological quest for national roots is extensively debated and inherent prejudices are examined dispassionately. Regionalism is seen as a countertrend to the universal force of Modern architecture and as a manifestation of identity. Quite a few architects of opposing persuasions in Southeast Asia have felt the urgent need for previously neglected

There is still much to marvel at among the extensive ruins of temple complexes in northern Thailand.

In places like Si Satchanalai and Sukhothai in northern Thailand, ruins of religious buildings reflect borrowings from many cultures like Mon, Singhalese and Khmer.

cultural introspection and the formulation of truly national or even regional identities in design.

"Vernacular architecture" is one of the most used yet least understood terms in the region. Vernacular structures, or "architecture without architects", provide many basic lessons for architects. These time-proven shelters are invariably built by anonymous local craftsmen with local techniques and materials. Such dwellings reflect the society's accumulated wisdom and collective images. They are imbued with cosmological and religious values, social and political structures, sensibility and attitude towards time and space. Their forms and proportions, craftsmanship and decorations, are symbolic and meaningful.

Much research has been done by scholars and anthropologists in the field of vernacular dwellings. Paul Oliver, Gaston Bachelard, Martin Heidegger, Amos Rapoport and Roxana Waterson are some of the important contributors who have given us greater insights into these indigenous structures. To Rapoport, "The folk tradition is the direct and unselfconscious translation into physical forms of a culture, its needs and values - as well as

the needs, dreams and passions of a people... The folk tradition is more closely related to the culture of the majority and life as it is really lived than is the grand design tradition which represents the culture of the elite."

In recent years, there has been a steady stream of architectural works emerging from Southeast Asian countries that refer back to some extent to their heritage and local realities. They try to recover the vital underpinnings that once linked architecture with the past. Some manage to abstract and reinvigorate the vitality of vernacular structures while others merely indulge in a romantic peasantism.

On the positive side, such approach enables countries confronting rapid changes to penetrate into the creative potential of pre-existing elements and build upon them. The negative aspect is that many architects opt for a facile approach of slavishly imitating past forms, reducing these traditional symbols into mere signs. In a consumer society, this nostalgic appropriation of picturesque relics easily degenerates into pastiches of cultural stereotypes. Such superficial mimicry is a sign of regressive sentimentalism, and this irrespon-

Traditional Thai dwellings are raised on stilts to protect the occupants from floods and animals. This structure is one of the best examples of Shan-influenced architecture.

Saddle-backed roofs of the Torajas in the highlands of the southwestern peninsula of Sulawesi, Indonesia.

sible concoction of bogus historicism can only result in hackneyed works.

Regionalism can be defined as a self-conscious commitment to uncover a particular tradition's unique response to place and climate, and thereafter exteriorise these formal and symbolic identities into creative new forms through an artist's eye that is very much in touch with contemporary realities and lasting human values. Only when we recognise that our tradition is a heritage that is evolving all the time will we be able to find the correct balance between regional and international identities. Architects need to decide which principles are still appropriate for today and how best to incorporate these with modern building requirements and current constructional methods.

The response to this context is crucial. What of the old is to be retained and what is to be rejected? Instead of viewing tradition and modernity as polar opposites that are mutually exclusive, they should be conceived as complementary in nature.

The word "tradition" originates from the Latin verb "trado-transdo", which essentially means "to pass on to another", or "to transmit possession". Tradition is thus seen as a dual process of preservation as well as transmission.

One is reminded of T. S. Eliot's theory of the relationship between tradition and novelty in his famous essay of 1919, "Tradition and the Individual Talent". Though Eliot's elucidation of the structure of relationship between quotation and invention was based on literature and poetry in particular, architecture shares a similar relationship. According to him, a true sense of tradition is a sense of the timeless and the temporal together. Eliot suggests that "Tradition... cannot be inherited, and if you want it you must obtain it by great labour. It involves in the first place, a historical sense, which... involves a perception, not only of the pastness of the past, but of its presence, ...The past should be altered by the present as much as the present is directed by the past... the difference between the present and the past is that the conscious present is an awareness of the past in a way and to an extent which the past's awareness of itself cannot show."

In a sea of commercial architecture, there are architects who are resolute in not sacrificing local traditions to the forces of modernisation. Significant regionalist

Designed to appeal to the intellect, the stupas on the upper terraces of Borobudur represent the pilgrim's expanded vision of the world.

The particularly striking Balinese pagoda, the "meru", was probably introduced from Java during the 14th century.

A temple courtyard at Bersakih, Bali.

works in different parts of the world demonstrate a high level of collaboration among architects and indigenous craftsmen. The late Mexican poet/architect Luis Barragán combined modernist planning with sensual architecture, which according to Ambasz, "results from a redemptive commitment to beauty." Hassan Fathy used the rural culture of Egypt for inspiration while closer to Southeast Asia, Geoffrey Bawa draws simple lessons from Sri Lanka's peasant vernacular architecture and other Southeast Asian prototypes which he sensitively combines to produce hauntingly eloquent works of architecture of high poetic intensity. In Southeast Asia, Australian architect Peter Muller has interwoven simplicity and complexity to create enthralling architecture at Amandari Resort in Bali. Vernacular details are assembled with sensitivity, rigour and understanding.

This can also be seen in Wija Wawo Runtu's evocative Tanjung Sari Hotel at Sanur Beach, where traditional elements deeply rooted in Bali's culture are presented in a highly condensed manner. Built at intervals between 1961 and 1978, Runtu has invested old truths with fresh vitality

and at the same time, made the vernacular respectable. In Phuket, Ed Tuttle's understanding of traditional Thai construction allows him to be adaptive and inventive in his subtle approach to the design of Amanpuri Resort.

In Malaysia, the critically acclaimed Tanjong Jara Beach Hotel and the Rantau Abang Visitor's Centre deserve special mention in that the architects use traditional forms and materials in a manner that captures the essence of Malaysian indigenous architectural types.

Malaysian architect Jimmy Lim's remarkable series of distinctive houses with intriguing variations also reflect his sincere effort to develop critical vernacular and regional forms that relate to the country's context. He believes that "architecture in Malaysia would have to be developed from observation of our environment, lifestyle, climate and more of what and who we are. One has to discover something that is first practical, that responds to the environment and the climate, and has a very traditional feeling about it in terms of materials that one uses - then people, all Malaysians, will identify with it." The importance of Lim's unique architecture resides in his sensitive interpretation of traditional forms and inevitably, his Precima House at Bangsar and the Eu House at Damansara exhibit all these concerns.

Many of the examples shown in the book are middle-class commissions. They include exclusive tourist resorts located in remote tropical environments. Some critics question the validity of these secluded enclaves of pleasure in the Third World environment when there are more pressing issues like low-cost housing, resettlement and rural planning.

Although these unabashedly hedonistic creations for the elite cannot claim to have tackled the issue of formulating a more pervasive and identifiable approach in design, the architectural strategy reintroduces and sustains certain traditional values. They provide ample evidence that the subtle blend of the new and the old can produce sensitive forms. These exemplary buildings also enable the local population to become cognizant of the inherent beguiling features of traditional built form, thus promoting greater public awareness of a rich vernacular heritage.

Together these architects have demonstrated that an exemplary architecture of place is the result of a poetic and allegorical way of thinking, in addition to sensitive transformation of past principles. They have shown that vernacular architecture is not simply an equation of utility and economy. Each of the works presented in this volume very much derives from the specifics of the site and the intricacies of local culture.

The finely proportioned "Bale Kambang" or "floating pavilion" at Klungkung, East Bali.

The exclusive resort of Amanpuri, which means "Place of Peace" in Sanskrit, is arguably one of Southeast Asia's best resorts. Located on the tranquil island of Phuket, Amanpuri comprises 40 secluded pavilions. The client, Adrian Zecha of Amanresorts, conceived it as a place that peddles paradise, yet retains a residential charm. Opened in 1988, it is an ideal setting for the carefree mind and contemplative spirit.

The light and elegant pavilions are dramatically set among leaning palms on a sprawling 40-hectare plot of a coconut plantation. The site rises steeply from the long horizontal sweep of Pansea Beach to an elevation of 40 metres. Grand steps descend from the resort to the crystal-clear sea.

The evocative formal language expressed in the pavilions sought inspiration in the traditional forms and techniques of Thai temple construction. Paris-based American architect Ed Tuttle's painstaking research was given a new light after visiting the finest gilded and decorated Buddhist temples of northern Thailand. His design is executed with fine control of the Thai vernacular of the Ayutthaya period, resulting in an architecture full of spatial effects that are both seductive and refined. The impact of the tropical idyll is immediate. Tuttle's other works include Adrian Zecha's private residences, the interiors of the Sukhothai Hotel in Bangkok and the Beaufort Hotel in Singapore.

Form and space reveal a hierarchy of intentions. The pavilions and the connecting walk-

Site plan, showing the layout of the entrance pavilion and the 40 private pavilion suites.

The resort is designed with derivatives from the local vernacular, extending the impulses of Thai architecture into new territories.
Previous page: At Amanpuri, the restful appearance of flat water lilies derives much of its visual strength from the contrast with the hard landscape.

Grand steps descend from the resort to Pansea Beach.

ways are supported by stilts to protect the land from erosion. Each pavilion consists of a bedroom unit incorporating a spacious bathroom, totalling about 100 sq m in size. An adjoining open-air "sala", or covered reception area, is linked by a verandah.

The picturesque high gable ends of the grey-tiled roofs are closed off by the distinctive design of the barge-board, the most poignant symbol of Thai architecture. Tuttle fully exploited the local craft traditions. The construction technology as well as the labour is local. All the veneer for the columns, mouldings and framing is of "maka", a local hardwood, while the floors are of another indigenous timber called "tabak". The monochromatic interior finishes also utilise local ma-

terials. Even the cotton fabrics are woven by the famous Jim Thompson factory in Bangkok.

The unsurpassed beauty of the resort is further enhanced by sensitive landscaping, with pools and lotus ponds surrounding the public pavilions and two restaurant buildings. Lined with blue black tiles, the centrally located swimming pool is a visual complement to the crystalline Andaman Sea.

Amanpuri offers compelling evidence that an invigorating pursuit of traditional archetypes can produce a graceful and totally engaging resort. A work of architecture like this one, meticulously crafted by skilled artisans, succeeds in achieving an ambience of serenity while demonstrating the poetic force of clear expression.

A view of one of the private villas. The bedroom unit is housed under the steeply pitched roof on the right while the living space is on the left.
Right: The verandah between the bedroom unit and the covered reception area, or "sala", is an ideal setting for the carefree mind and contemplative spirit.

Since its beginnings in the 1950s, Club Mediterranee has successfully promoted the French holiday idea of mixing leisure with sports. From 1970, the resort empire's expansion began to establish itself in the tropical isles of Tahiti, Mauritius and Maldives. In 1980, its first vacation village in Southeast Asia opened in the Malaysian east coast of Cherating. Recently, two new additions were established in Phuket and Bali.

The Club Med resort on Kata Beach in the southwest corner of Phuket Island opened in 1986. Nestled among 36 lush hectares of coconut plantations, the Club consists of clusters of double-storey traditionally-styled buildings radiating out from a huge central complex. Architect M L Tri Devakul is one of Thailand's leading contemporary architects, having designed several hotels in Phuket, among them the luxurious Phuket Yacht Club and the Phuket Meridien.

Opened in December 1988, Club Med Bali is widely regarded as the most spectacular Club Med village. Situated on a 14-hectare site, it is the work of architects Christian Demonchy of Noelle Janet-Christian Demonchy Architecture and Decoration. Although a huge complex — with 402 rooms in low-rise blocks radiating from a spine — the architecture is the epitome of thoughtful integration of building to site and romantic response to Balinese architecture. The architect used as much of local materials as possible. The wonderfully lush landscaping consists of plants chosen for their unique colourful blooms and foliage character. This bold display of luminous foliage provide a wonderful setting for the visual enjoyment of the sensitive architecture.

View of the entrance pavilion at Club Med Phuket.

The design is a synthesis of traditional forms with present day sensibilities.

Single-storey pavilions enclose a water-filled court at the entrance lobby.

Major elements of tropical architecture - pitched roofs, landscape design, water features, courtyards, in-between realms and use of materials - are all handled with sensitivity at Club Med Bali.

*Timber is used at the highest level, in contrast to the
masonry structure at the lower levels.*

The lobby lounge of Amanusa overlooks the expansive blue-tiled swimming pool.

Amanusa, located in Nusa Dua, Bali, commands spectacular views of the island of Nusa Penida. Designed by Singapore-based Kerry Hill Architects, the resort is made up of a total of 35 individual pavilion suites linked to the public facilities by a series of pathways. The exterior areas of each pavilion include a walled forecourt, a private courtyard with a sunken bath in a reflecting pool, and a spacious living area beneath a pergola. Most of the facilities like the bar, restaurant, shop, gallery and library are located in the main two-storey building.

Through deft manipulation of massing and materials, the architects have created an architectural ensemble in a direct and unaffected manner. Rubble walls give a powerful sense of permanence. Clearly recognising those qualities endemic to the local design precepts, the architects simply take the ordinary and do it extraordinarily well. The result is a sensual architecture of intimate scale that provides an excellent model for a future source of inspiration.

The resort, seen from the adjacent golf course, is a sprawling, low-impact complex.

View of the monumental double-storey block from the outdoor dining terrace.

A series of lotus-filled jars and water spouts lined the pool.

The pervasive use of random rubble walls provides a strong sense of permanence.

A typical covered walkway connecting various parts of the main building.

The allure of the pool provides an essential visual complement to the landscape.

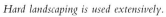

Hard landscaping is used extensively.   *The design of the pavilion suites is based on traditional Balinese villages.*

The pavilion suites nestle among sensitively designed gardens, some of which are carefully planned beds of "alang-alang", the material that is commonly used as roof finishes in Bali.

Australian architect Peter Muller took full advantage of the enchanting qualities of Bali to conceive the sybaritic haven of the luxurious Amandari Resort. Managed by Amanresorts and owned by P T Villa Ayu, Amandari's associated hotels include the famous Amanpuri in Phuket as well as Amankila and Amanusa in Bali.

Officially opened in December 1989, the intimate and low-key resort is located in picturesque Ubud, away from the overcrowded tourist belt. This town on the southern flank of the central mountains of Bali has been a haven for artists since the 1920s. In many ways Ubud resembles an extended village and is home to numerous talented musicians, dancers and wood carvers. The resort's raison d'etre is definitely its excellent setting, resting at 80 metres above the perennially lush Ayung River gorge.

The special nature of the site also deserves mention. During the fifth century, a great sage in India was supposedly asked by an angel to follow a ball of blue light to Bali. It landed at the gorge below the site at a great spring. Amandari thus means "peace and heavenly beings". For the last 1,500 years, villagers visited this sacred site in a massive procession every six months.

Since the 1960s, Muller has been developing a site-specific and bio-climatically responsive architecture in his projects. In recent years, he was involved in the design of several resort hotels in Tahiti, Egypt and many parts of Southeast Asia, including the Bali Oberoi in Seminyak.

He likes to tell the architectural story by involving as many of the senses as possible, utilising objects and elements for their sounds, features, fragrances as well as their visual impact. These principal concerns of his are further illustrated in a compelling manner at Amandari.

The design of Amandari is based on the traditional Balinese village of wall-lined lanes and intimate courtyards. Muller's achievement is the creation of a tightly controlled sequence of indoor and outdoor spaces related to the surviving vernacular but reinterpreted to suit the larger scale of a new programme. The architect has designed 27 walled pavilions laid out brilliantly from the stand-point of the surrounding scale and integrated with the adjacent rice-terraced village of Kedewatan.

The design of Amandari is based on the traditional Balinese village of wall-lined lanes and intimate courtyards.

Two stone guardian figures flank one of the many pathways in the resort. The checked material draped on them ("saput poleng") is considered to have magical power to ward off evil-doers.

Each pavilion suite is carefully sited. A tribute to timeless craftsmanship is assured by the fine handling of proportions and details.

One of the two pavilion suites with its own private pool.

Gateway to the pavilion suite.

Muller has created a tightly controlled sequence of indoor and outdoor spaces related to the surviving vernacular.

Each pavilion has a living area of 100-150 sq m. This casually encountered structure draws on both the tangible and intangible sources of Balinese culture. The most obvious architectural theme is the rustic elemental style suggested by the pavilion's steeply pitched roof. Each is a thatched canopy with deep overhangs in the Balinese tradition. Tectonically, this pavilion suite is a clear expression of materials and construction, revealing the existence of a poetry of order at the same time.

In 16 duplex pavilion suites, a spiral staircase leads to the bedroom above. All suites also feature a sunken outdoor bath enclosed by high walls. Two duplexes have their own private swimming pool. The furniture and fabrics are supplied by local firms and designed with great restraint by Australian Neville Marsh. The sensitive integration of lush greenery with tectonic forms is the work of landscape architect Michael White, who is also known by his Balinese name, Made Wijaya.

In the words of Peter Muller, "Amandari, like the Oberoi, is honest architecture. Its integrity rests on the truth of its structure and materials. Nothing is fake. The construction technology is exactly what you see, extremely beautiful in its naturalness, its natural materials and human craftsmanship."

In every respect, Amandari, the "Abode of Tranquility" is an affectionate ode to the enigmatic landscape of Bali. Deceptively simple, it is one of those truly beguiling works of poetry that give the tropics so much of its allure. To quote Muller again: "Having lived on site, working 7 days a week, 10 hours a day for the 18 months it took to build Amandari, it is for me the full expression of my beliefs in how to build, as a non-Balinese in Bali. I have expressed and exhausted all I know about building in Bali and therefore do not wish to do so again, as it would only be repetitious."

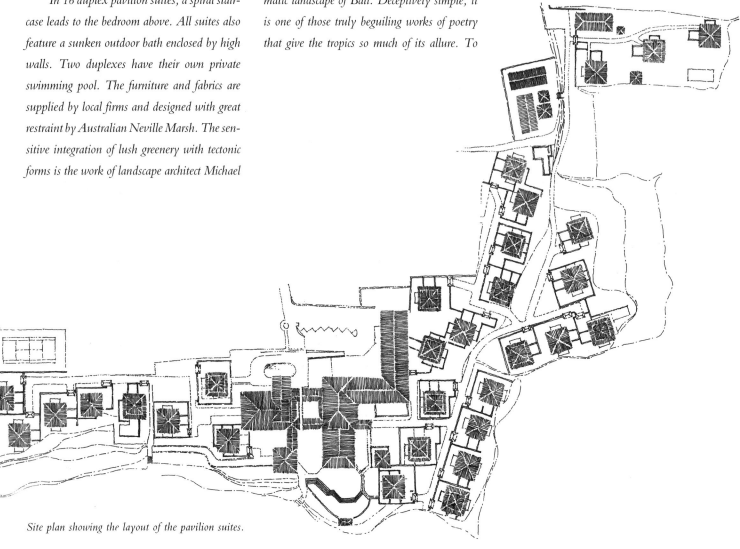

Site plan showing the layout of the pavilion suites.

Each pavilion draws on both the tangible and intangible sources of Balinese culture. It consists of a spacious sitting area opening out to private gardens.

A stone figurine in an open courtyard.

Tandjung Sari

Constructed wholly in vernacular forms, Tandjung Sari ("Cape of Flowers") is one of the most intimate and exquisitely beautiful resorts in Bali. It derives its name from a temple of the same name in Sanur beach. Created by Wija Wawo Runtu, owner and architect, Tandjung Sari is drawn extensively from the local idiom.

The serene retreat opened in 1962 as a four-bungalow extension to Wawo Runtu's family house. Today, there are 29 bungalows in all, laid out like a Balinese village. Set among rambling pathways and enigmatic gardens, each of the secluded double-storey bungalow has enclosed courtyards hidden behind high coral walls with a double bedroom on the second storey. The village suites are arranged in swastika-shaped clusters of four units each. Grey "alang-alang" (long grass) thatched roofs combined with red brickwork and natural timber finishes to provide an evocative image of unerring exactitude, while the direct relationship of the architecture with the elements generate a mood of uninvaded calm. Balinese arts and crafts and Dutch colonial antiques are everywhere. Tandjung Sari is a prime example of a building that derives its being from the synthesis of a poetic vision and the clarity of intention. The resultant richly allusive vocabulary, manifested through the simplest acts, provides evidence of a deft touch.

Wawo Runtu' son, Agus, now manages the hotel. An anthropologist by training, he started the Tandjung Sari Foundation which sponsors the young dancers of Sanur and the gamelan orchestra of Sindhu Karja village.

Site plan showing the layout of the pavilion suites.

Designed with derivatives from the local vernacular, Tandjung Sari demonstrates that the vernacular can be sensitively adapted to create a new synthesis and not used as mere pastiche.

The main reception pavilion,
where materials are appreciated
for their appearance and tactility.

This private courtyard is perfect for its meditative tranquility

A resting pavilion becomes a sybaritic enclave.

"The separate bungalows were built in native style and set in opulent gardens... statues of gods and goddesses appeared in niches. The room, with its split bamboo walls, mats, rafts, poles tied together with bark fibre, gave off vibrations which I can only describe as similar to those one feels in a forest, as if natural materials never lost their power to conduct life..."

- Tandjung Sari, as seen in "The Diary of Anais Nin, 1966-1974," published by Harcourt Brace Jovanovich Inc.

The village suites are arranged in "swastika" - shaped clusters of four units each, creating a central courtyard effect.

Each pavilion suite, set among rambling pathways and enigmatic gardens, demonstrates an elegant sense of restraint and refined proportion.

Scattered throughout the lush gardens are enigmatic stone figures, like this fountain. Simple acts provide evidence of a deft touch.

Rantau Abang Visitor's Centre and
Tanjong Jara Beach Hotel

Located on the east coast of Malaysia, 65 km south of Kuala Trengganu, this complex was one of the winners in the Aga Khan Awards for Architecture in 1983. Instituted in 1980, the triennial Awards seek to heighten awareness of Islamic culture while emphasising great value on the social, cultural and environmental aspects of architecture.

Master Jury's Citation: "For the courage to search out and successfully adapt and develop an otherwise rapidly disappearing traditional architecture and craft, and at the same time meet the demands of contemporary architecture. The programme, while attempting to provide a resort facility in an otherwise undeveloped area, is part of a broader strategy for the development of local architecture and the economy. In this, the project has succeeded by providing employment at the resort and at the industries that service the resort. Through the use of traditional architectural forms and materials, the project has revived a number of building-material industries, crafts and traditional constructional skills.

Though architecturally the adaptation of traditional forms to new uses raises several technical and ideological problems, the consistency with which this approach has been pursued in all levels of design and execution has generated an architecture that is in keeping with traditional values and aesthetics and of an excellence that matches the best surviving traditional examples."

The architects, Wimberly Whisenand Allison Tong and Goo of Hawaii with Akitek Bersekutu of Malaysia, have done an excellent job in integrating the architecture with the culture of the picturesque Malaysian east coast. Although the hotel and Visitor's Centre are 10 km apart, they are designed as part of an integrated whole.

The hotel consists of 100 guests rooms dispersed in small blocks and bungalows while the Visitor's Centre has a museum and 11 individual chalets. Both are inspired by some of the best features of Malaysian indigenous architecture, especially the century-old istanas, hardwood palaces built by the early kings. The resort is constructed of native hardwood, using a post-and-beam construction in the ethnic style. Eave carvings, gable screens and other decorative motifs are handcrafted by local artisans and integrated into the design. The result is a handsomely detailed resort of great confidence and competence, where site, form and materials have been integrated into an indissoluble whole.

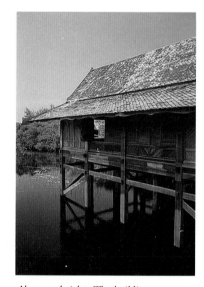

Above and right: The buildings at Rantau Abang Visitor's Centre are raised on stilts above the river to avoid disrupting the site's natural topography and ecology.

Rantau Abang's individual chalets are inspired by century-old hardwood palaces built by the early kings.

The two-storey hardwood constructed buildings at Tanjong Jara Beach Hotel each have 8 to 12 guest rooms. Placed in clusters, they are oriented towards the sea.

An intricate timber bridge spans the lagoon at Tanjong Jara.

The huge shettering roof of the reception pavilion at Tandjung Sari, Bali, is an exercise in form simplicity.

Roofs

"One unchanging element of all

building is the roof – protective,

emphatic, and all important...

Ubiquitous, pervasively present,

the scale or pattern shaped by

the building beneath. The roof,

its shape, texture and proportion

is the strongest visual factor."

- Geoffrey Bawa

A dominant element of architectural composition, the roof system of a building acts as the main protective device sheltering the spaces beneath from the natural elements. It also plays a primal role in our lives by giving people a fundamental sense of shelter and territory.

The most primitive building form in Southeast Asia is simply a great umbrella, an enormous roof over a raised platform that keeps out the sun and the rain. Walls are not really necessary as sheltering elements in the tropics, unlike in the Western world. The form of the roof system, while derived from a response to place and climate, also adds immeasurably to the architectural character and silhouette of the building.

The 'visible roof' is one of the critical elements that is a determinant of form. It gives distinction and interest, and provides the quickest visual impression of a distinctly regional flavour. Largely ignored in modern architecture, it is immediately perceivable at the level of the senses, as they reflect in a direct manner the scope and use of the building.

Studies have shown that the roof is an important symbol of the home. The pitched roof, especially, has primordial emotional roots. It is found to be the element most closely associated with the symbol of shelter and security. The North Americans and Northern Europeans have chosen to make the run-off of rain and snow the major determinant of the roof's form. In the tropics, the traditional pitched roofs quickly and efficiently remove the torrential downpour and provide generous space to the interior in which the high ceiling is ideal for inducing air movements and cross-ventilation. This ubiquitous roof form, with its strong massing endlessly repeated in natural materials more or less in the same manner as craftsmen have always done it, is still very much a dominant theme in contemporary architecture in Southeast

The roof provides the quickest visual impression of a distinctly regional flavour, like this roof form which is typical of Balinese rice barns.

The striking 'meru', a Balinese pagoda representing the cosmic mountain Mahameru, always has an odd number of tiered roofs.

Grey "alang-alang" thatched roofs provide an evocative image at the Four Seasons Resort in Bali.

Corner detail of a typical Balinese thatched roof. An extra thickness of thatch is always added to the four corners.

Asia. Distinctive triangular roof sections are formed by using diagonal members of timber or bamboo.

Throughout Southeast Asia, there are houses physically raised high on stilts or piles with expressive pitched roofs conceptualised in a great number of ways. Most of them are derivatives of the gable roof. Historically, this architecture is linked to the "water people" and their way of life. Research indicates that in an area starting from the far eastern islands of the Indonesian Archipelago to Sumatra, the Malay Peninsula, Indo-China and Yunnan, there is a particular house-type raised high on stilts. They have saddle-backed roofs and outward-sloping gable ends that relate to the form of reed boats turned upside-down.

These beautifully carved and richly decorated designs, built by the Sa'dan Torajas and the Minangkabaus, can still be seen today in the highlands of the southwestern peninsula of Sulawesi (once known as the Celebes) and Sumatra. The Toraja people, still preserving elements of late neolithic Southeast Asian culture, wear ceremonial head-dresses which resemble the structurally daring roofs of their unique dwellings.

The hypothesis about the origins of these upswept roof forms is that when Pro-Malay races of the region navigated across the seas from the continent in the Indochinese Peninsula in old times to the islands of Southeast Asia, they used their boats turned upside-down as the roofs. Engravings of structures resembling Toraja houses were found on bronze drums dating back to 500 B.C. in the northern coast of Vietnam, suggesting common roots during late neolithic times.

However, anthropologist Roxanna Waterson believes the thesis proposing that such imposing roofs actually symbolised the original boats of migrants may now be seen as simplistic and improbable. She points out that some academicians have suggested that the evidence has been

The most primitive building form in Southeast Asia is simply a great umbrella, an enormous roof over a raised platform that keeps out the elements.

Club Med Bali has been designed to create a traditional Balinese-style structure with hand-carved timber roof tiles and walls of ochre-red bricks. The roofs cascade over the four levels to create a more intimate scale.

The form of the roof system, while derived from a response to place and climate, also adds immeasurably to the architectural character and silhouette of the building as seen in this night scene at the Grand Hyatt Bali.

exaggerated by anthropologists keenly looking for "boat" associations. In her book, "The Living House", she quotes recent scholars like Gittinger (1976) and Manguin (1986), who "have proposed much more convincing explanations of the recurring use of boat symbolism simply as a convenient organising metaphor for expressing various ideas of social order or representing moments of transition. Another major problem with the older approach lies in the very notion of anything so coherent as a megalithic culture in Indonesia".

The symbolic importance of the water buffalo in Southeast Asian societies also deserves a mention. This animal, which signifies wealth, prestige, strength and virility is used as a recurring architectural motif by the Bataks of Sumatra. These Karo Batak houses have roof finials that resemble the buffalo's horns. The Toraja houses, especially those belonging to aristocrats, are often adorned with a carved buffalo head attached with real horns. The Northern Thai house, popularly called a "kalae", has prominent crossed gable-finials that resembles a buffalo's body. Similar explicit depictions can be found among the houses of the Simalungun Batak of Sumatra.

Another common roof form is the pyramidal roof which ranges from simple dwellings and house shrines in Bali to elaborately tiered mosques in the Malay Peninsula. This *bumbung limas* roof is seldom used for residences. The Balinese roof is a hipped pavilion called a *bale,* which is covered by thatch (*alang-alang*) and always crowned by a terracotta finial. In the words of Miguel Covarrubias, "A well-built bale, the archetype of Balinese construction, is a masterpiece of simplicity, ingenuity and good taste". Variations of the pavilion form can also be found on the islands of Melanesia and Polynesia. They have been modified to achieve unique identities and are variously known as fale, fare, vale, whare and bure.

The striking *meru*, a Balinese pagoda representing the cosmic heavenly mountain Mahameru, has an odd number of roofs, from three to a maximum of 11. Each type is dedicated to a different deity. This sanctified roof form is a distinctive element of sacred buildings in Java too.

Detail of a timber roof truss.

A complex timber trussed roof at the Bali Hilton.

Steeply pitched roofs create a voluminous interior at The Oberoi Bali.

Different types of roof trusses are employed in the design of large-span structures for the lobbies of many recent hotels in Bali.

Slender bodies of "naga" are usually found on the gable ends of Thai roofs.

Most Westerners are also familiar with the lofty Thai temples topped by sloping multi-tiered roofs with ornately decorated gable-ends. Rearing serpent heads at the corners of the eaves and the horn-like gold-finished, slender finial known as the *chofa* (sky tassel) at the ridge apex are other characteristics of the graceful Thai roof. This structure is said to resemble the *garuda*, a divine bird always seen grasping two nagas with its claws. Buildings cannot be regarded as sacred until the *chofa* has been positioned in its rightful place.

In Peninsular Malaysia, distinct regional variations of the Malay dwellings are classified by their roof shapes. Several types of domestic architecture can be identified, like the "Minangkabau" house, the "Kelantan" house and the "Bugis" house. Each has its unique roof form. The simplest but most highly developed of these roofs is *bumbung panjang*, a gable roof supported by king posts. The use of ventilation grilles at its gable ends allows for efficient cross-ventilation. The *bunga matahari*, a motif of radiating sun rays, is a common feature found on the gable ends.

Roofing materials in Southeast Asian buildings are sympathetically chosen and detailed with great skill. They can be placed in two distinct groups. One is cheap, durable and can be easily prepared from natural materials with simple tools while the other is imported and industrially produced. The former group includes thatching materials like native grasses, reeds and shingles while the latter consists of unglazed terracotta roofing tiles, commonly known as Marseilles tiles, and the less common slate. Native grasses are cut in small bunches and folded over bamboo strips which are attached to the rafters. The grey *alang-alang* (long grass) is ubiquitous

Much of the elegant loftiness of traditional Thai architecture is due to the elaborate muilt-tiered roofs, like this structure, Wat Chong Kham of Lampang.

Right: Liltingly curved gableboards of Amanpuri's multi-tiered roof charm through their appealing verve.
Overleaf: The elegant interior of the reception lobby of Amanpuri is especially dramatic at night. A richness of effect is achieved through the roof trusses, fine scale and elegant details.

This Lanna-style "wihan" of Wat Chieng Khong in the province of Chiengrai is widely recognised as the finest surviving example of Thai timber architecture.

A typical roof of the Thai house, in the style of the Central Plains region.

Wat Chong Kham of Lampang. The roof's structure demonstrates the delicate wood-carving skills of northern Thai craftsman.

The distinctive pitched roofs of Thailand's traditional domestic architecture.

Gilded finials grace Thai temple roofs.

to Bali. Cut in the holiest month of *Saseh Kedasa* (around May), it is thoroughly dried before used in such manner. Good quality alang-alang is said to able to last at least 20 years.

In traditional Malay domestic architecture, the common roofing materials are *nipah*, *rumbia* (sago) or *bertam* thatch. In northern Thailand, teak tiles are also used. The structural members consists of either bamboo or different varieties of hard wood timber, especially teak. However, certain woods like the *yon* tree in Thailand are taboo because it is believed that spirits reside in them. The spacing, span and slope of these structural members influence the choice of the finished materials. They also affect the layout and form of the interior spaces as well as the ceiling system. Durability, economy of erection and maintenance, and potential heat gain

are factors which are considered in the choice of a roof system.

Not all roof forms that touch our imagination are exotic, nor need they all be complex. Throughout history, the roof is the most variable element in architecture and has received an infinite number of interpretations, from one of formal dignity to that of lyric spontaneity. The diversified expression, when created through the most attentive elaboration of the parts, always enrich our perception. This aesthetic play in structure is an important aspect of building in Southeast Asia. Sensitive contemporary architects of the region have expressed in the silhouette of their works a sense of the poetry of the tropics and a sincere search for expressions within the heritage of local building cultures that will truly enhance the places they occupy.

Contemporary interpretation of traditional roof forms. This pair of houses in Singapore by William Lim Associates, have elegant roofs that provide ample shade and make a strong visual statement at the same time.

An "umbrella" roof truss system in Pansea Beach Resort, Phuket, Thailand.

Roof trusses at Pelangi Beach Resort, Malaysia.

Exposed roof members at the entrance porch, Tanjang Jara Beach Resort, Malaysia.

Eave carvings, gable screens and other decorative motifs are painstakingly handcrafted by local artisans in many resorts, like the Pelangi in Malaysia.

Roof detail of one of the chalets at Tanjong Jara. The gable end forms a bargeboard called "tepang layar". Right: The roof forms at Club Med Cherating are inspired by some of the best features of Malaysian indigenous architecture, especially the hardwood palaces built by the early kings of the east coast.

This serenely contained house occupies a site at the top of a steep slope in Kuala Lumpur, Malaysia. One of the winners of the PAM (Malaysian Institute of Architects) Architectural Awards in 1989, the building's value lies in its demonstration that architect Jimmy Lim's work bridges the gap between tradition and contemporary living. Built in traditional timber as well as reinforced concrete, the house is basically planned around a central pool. A large living area crowned by a large "umbrella-roof" forms the most impressive part of the house. Living and dining spaces are open to the cool breezes. The ambiguous relationship between inside and outside, and the lush landscaping combine to provide an atmosphere of serenity and seclusion essential for a dwelling.

The "umbrella-roof", as seen from the garden.

View of the timber columns that support the main roof.

The high-volume living area of the Precima House is crowned by a large "umbrella-roof".

The Eu House in Kuala Lumpur, Malaysia, is an exciting concoction of constructional surprises.

Eu House

Winner of the coveted PAM (Malaysian Institute of Architects) Architectural Awards 1989 in the single residential building category, the Eu House is an architecturally sophisticated piece of work, displaying the intricate geometry of interesting roof planes one usually associates with Jimmy Lim's oeuvre. The house, a tour de force of imaginative siting and built on a land area comprising some 800 sq m, stands poised above the steep spur of a hill in the suburb of Damansara, Kuala Lumpur.

A cascade of levels run down the hill, with stilts lifting them off the ground to address the excellent view. Security is handled in a hierarchical manner, starting from the entry level at the upper road. The overall layout is based on a deftly orchestrated structural system. The first storey houses a central staircore and a carporch with family and study rooms on each side. The second storey contains three bedrooms while the floor below the entry is occupied by the kitchen and dining areas. Besides holding the spaces together, the central staircore plays a pivotal role as a strong circulation element as well as providing the support for the provocative radiating roof.

The central staircore supports the radiating main roof.

The house cascades down the steep terrain with a deftly orchestrated series of roof forms.

Completed in February 1990, this house at Ridout Road, Singapore, by William Lim Associates draws its sources of inspiration partly from the black-and-white bungalows built by the British during colonial days. It is basically made up of three carefully composed blocks: an imposing two-level front block with a hipped roof; a family block overlooking the swimming pool; and a service block which houses the kitchen and the yard. Natural finishes of fair-faced bricks and wide over-hanging eaves lend it its intended tropical look. Red balau timber columns left in their natural state further contribute to the interplay of structure and foliage, light and shade. Yet this is a house which is flavoured throughout by a contemporary feel, which the architect hopes will signal "the time period so that it would continue to be relevant to both present and future generations". This is distinctly enhanced by the use of contemporary materials like steel in some of the original details as well as the tilting of grids on plan, which hints at the shifted axes and skewed grids common to some American projects. However, this unlikely combination all come together in a satisfactory whole.

Timber columns support the roof of the main block.

The main block of the house has ten two-storey high circular timber columns supporting the main pyramidal roof, which projects beyond the core concrete structure.

Paradisiacal private domain of a beautifully landscaped garden designed by Michael White at Villa Bebek, Bali.

Landscape and Gardens

"A garden is a construction, like a novel by Dostoevsky or Tolstoy. They knew how to capture a climate, to dramatize certain moments, to emphasize. It's the same thing in a garden: how you conduct the spectator to see the same thing from different angles."

- Burle Marx

Densely planted beds in a sensitively nurtured garden provide a backdrop to the pool.

The construction and enjoyment of a garden accustoms people to beauty, to its instinctive use, even to its pursuit." - Luis Barragán.

Throughout most of the 20th century, little emphasis was placed on gardens, thus depriving man a large part of his sense of the sublime. This is unfortunate because the garden has its own poetics and spiritual underpinnings. It has been intimately linked to man and the inhabited environment from early times, evoking a mythical and poetic order that touches the soul.

Man's notion of the Paradise myth envisions paradise as a lush and eternal garden — an enduring expression of man's relationship to nature and the cosmos. The Chinese and Japanese have attempted to reflect the order of the planets in the cosmos within the ordered microcosm of their miniaturised gardens of enchantment. This "heaven-on-earth" has never been more profoundly realised than in Katsura Palace, where a ceremonial hierarchical progression through the spaces reveal a gradual corresponding comprehension of the cosmos. It is truly a confrontation with nature in the widest possible sense. Oriental gardens and those of 15th century Mughal India were conceived in a similar manner. They were seen as inseparable from the architecture to which they formed an integral part.

In the tropics, buildings are not mere objects in the landscape. Shaded gardens provide great relief in the hot climate while

Plants are used in architectural place-making in the tropics to create a strong sense of place and primordial presence.

An outdoor patio at Villa Bebek. Luxuriant tropical exotics provide screening as well as heighten the atmosphere of the setting.

In Bali, some of the most beautiful tropical gardens can be found in the private Batujimbar Estates.

Traditional stone figures of the Hanuman god can be found in many Balinese gardens.

plants soften hard building edges. Architecturally, gardens provide a crucial zone in terms of spatial hierarchy, acting as an intermediate space between the private and the public realms. From the most intimate gardens to the majestic royal grounds, they offer delights not just with their colour, form and compositional arrangement, but also through their fragrance and essentially contemplative qualities. Gardens created out of a mixture of extreme sensitivity for plants and an expressed desire to complement buildings evoke different moods at different times of the day. A sense of place and primordial presence is strongly elicited.

Plants are used in architectural placemaking to define space, provide privacy, frame views and create exciting spatial sequences. They also have a perceptible effect on the micro-climate of the surroundings, acting as an absorbent material, reducing heat, glare and airborne noise. Trees planted strategically are not only visually pleasing, but also provide efficient shade and act as wind barriers.

In Brazil, Robert Burle-Marx has done much to raise the public's consciousness of the dramatic nature and beauty of tropical flora, opening up new vistas into the discipline. Inspired by contemporary abstract painters, his post-Cubist landscapes blend mythic evocations with the tactile sensuality of the landscape. He conceived his gardens (at least 600 designed or built) in terms of form, texture, colour and even

Water plants are unique because they always contribute a special mood to any garden. Cultivated mainly for its flowers, the lotus is probably the most spectacular of all water plants.

aural effects. The latter was manifested through his choice of plants with acoustic resonance when rustled by the wind, and in his constant use of moving water. In fact, quite a number of plants have been named after Burle-Marx, for example, the *Heliconia burle-marxii*. Another trademark of Burle-Marx is his avoidance of mixing several varieties of plants in a single plot. Not surprisingly, he is widely considered to be the strongest single influence on tropical landscaping, leaving an indelible influence on many of the landscape architects practising in Southeast Asia today.

The number of plant species both native and imported in Southeast Asia available to a landscape designer is staggering. The fertile region is truly remarkable for the amazing wealth and overwhelming diversity of its plant forms. A luxuriant profusion of tropical foliage pro-

vided an abundant source of food medicine and other necessities for the local people. The vegetation is also conditioned by soil types, precipitation and altitude. Early Western voyagers came to the opulent region in search of natural resources, especially the rich spices, while naturalists were captivated by the visual impact of exotic species of flora and fauna. Notable travellers, including the famous Victorian naturalist Alfred Russel Wallace, Arthur Adams and Hugh Low, were spellbound by the unique forms and colours of the varied vegetation.

In addition, many foreign species of plants have been introduced through the centuries. They have thrived very well, further augmenting the indigenous stock of luxuriant flora. However, there was no tradition of ornamental horticulture among the locals. It was mainly the Euro-

Lushly landscaped grounds of Poppies' Cottages in Kuta, Bali.

Grouped in large masses, the different varieties of plants form exciting patterns and textures in the garden of Poppies' Cottages.

Stone carvings created by local artisans further complement the sense of tropical luxuriance in this landscaped garden at Nusa Dua, Bali.

Water jets add to the cool serenity of the gardens at Nusa Dua.

The exquisitely landscaped tropical gardens of Sheraton Senggigi Beach Resort in Lombok, Indonesia, designed by Bill Bensley, is further complemented by deft touches of details that are both sensual and witty, like the 'geckos' on the columns.

peans who introduced the western concept of landscape design. Traditional rural settlements consist of well-developed private gardens with fruit trees, bamboo and herbal plants grown in the vicinity of the dwellings. Spices such as chilli, lemon grass, pepper, ginger and mint are commonly cultivated.

Traditionally, flowers play an important role in religious ceremonies and other auspicious occasions. Intricate floral arrangements and plaited banana leaves are also made for domestic uses as well as for royal purposes. In Bali, daily presentation of offerings (*banten*) consists of elaborately plaited leaves and attractive varieties of flowers. The colours of these flowers are related to the gods, like red for Brahma, black or green for Vishnu and white for Shiva. In Thailand, floral arrangements around the food is known as *baisi-pakcham*.

Water plants are unique because they always contribute a special mood to any garden. Probably the most spectacular of all water plants are the lotus and the different species of water-lilies of the *Nymphae* family. Many people are confused over

the difference between the two although the distinction is very obvious. The former has umbrella-shaped leaves and can be as large as 30 cm in diameter. They rise on tall stalks above the water surface while the leaves of the water-lily floats on water. Also, the lotus flowers have an inverted cone in the centre and are also raised on tall stalks while the flowers of the water-lily have very short stalks.

According to Hindu beliefs, the lotus is venerated as a symbol of the Ganges and also as a life-giving symbol. Brahma, the Hindu god of creation, is believed to have been born from a lotus in Vishnu's navel, while Vishnu's consort, Lakshmi, is said to have emerged from another lotus on Vishnu's forehead. The aquatic lotus also plays an important symbolic role in Buddhism, as reflected in the classical architecture of the region. Details of joints and decorative parts in the columns of temples are frequently derived from the lotus motif. In fact, the Thai word for "moulding" is the same as for "lotus". Cultivated mainly for its flowers, the lotus is native to many parts of Asia. The most common variety is

The compounds of Club Med Bali are densely planted with ground covers, lotus, ferns, palms and other carefully sited sculptural objects.

An arcadian retreat in a superb scenographic setting, Amandari's gardens are a pleasure to behold.

the species with pink flowers.

One of the most prevalent plants in Southeast Asia is the palm. There are more than ten times as many varieties of palms in tropical Asia than in Africa, and the species range from the tall majestic sealing wax palm to the ubiquitous coconut — numerous products are made from virtually every part of this plant. Another common plant that is used for making all kind of artefacts is the highly adaptable bamboo. Frangipani (*Plumeria*) is also widely grown in the region, especially in Bali, and is often found in temples and cemeteries in other parts of Southeast Asia. The plant is treasured for its thick, angular branches, highly defined leaves and the scent of its colourful blooms. Like many other ornamental plants, the three common species of frangipani were introduced from tropical America to Southeast Asia by the Spanish. Their popularity can also be at-

tributed to the fact that they are easily grown by stem cutting. However, it is taboo in Thailand because its Thai name, "lantom" sounds very similar to "ratom", which means "misfortune".

Yet another common group is the family of ferns. The bird's nest fern (*Asplenium nidus*), is one of the world's largest fern genera and can be found in virtually all of Southeast Asia. The *heliconias*, the lesser known relative of the banana, are frequently cultivated by gardeners for the great beauty of their flowers. Orchids also have a special place among Southeast Asia flora. The number of species totals 27,000. They are often regarded as most characteristic of tropical plants, and many consider them to be the most beautiful of all flowers.

In Bali, some of the most beautiful tropical gardens can be found in the private Batujimbar Estates in Sanur. Land-

Stone steps leading to the pool.

Landscape architect Micheal White has imparted a distinct character to the grounds of Amandari. His concept was based on "classic Balinese romantic courtyards".

Statuary and other garden ornaments control and manipulate the visual cues in a garden.

scape architect Bill Bensley of Bill Bensley Design Group International has been involved in the planning and construction of many of these ever-evolving gardens since 1986. He has completed four residences in Batujimbar — Kajima Estate, House A, Frank Morgan's Wantilan Lama and Adrian Zecha's Pura Muntik.

His signature is the creation of vivid imagery and a strong sense of place by incorporating specific knowledge of a culture, its people and their art into each project. Designing tropical gardens as a series of vignettes or individual stories, Bensley's approach can best be summed up by his statement that "beauty is created when there is no clear, expected boundary. Tropical architecture should embrace the landscape, and invite it into its deepest rooms."

Australian landscape designer Michael White has also taken advantage of the extraordinary repertory of flora to enrich his gorgeous Balinese gardens with grace and evocative effects. Artfully sculpted out of the lush foliage and furnished with delightful statuary and other anthropomorphic objects, White's tropical havens are full of surprises. They are a blend of controlled wilderness and unexpected discoveries.

Frangipani ("jepun jawa"), an integral part of Balinese culture, is extensively used in contemporary resorts, like the Four Seasons Resort at Jimbaran.

Ecological reverence is clearly evident in the attempt at integrating structure and nature.

The pavilions and gardens are conceived as a series of Balinese villages tucked into the hillside, overlooking Jimbaran Bay, a crescent-shaped cove with six-kilometres of sandy beach.

A huge lotus pond acts as the focal point in this Balinese compound at Sanur. Called Taman Mertasari, or "Garden of Holy Water Essence", it consists of several attractive pavilions designed around an open garden.

A thatched-roof rice barn at Taman Mertasari. Existing coconut palms were incorporated into the landscape design when the compound was built.

Bali Hyatt

Opened in November 1973, the 387-room Bali Hyatt is located in Sanur, a former fishing village and home to Brahman priests. It was built on a former coconut plantation of over 2000 trees. Designed by the Hong Kong firm, Palmer and Turner, the simple architecture is successfully integrated into 15 hectures of spectacular landscaped gardens. There is a clear expressiveness in the use of architectural elements. Wide overhanging eaves contribute to the pronounced horizontality that creates a close relationship to the ground. Wild gardens overflowing with frangipani trees, bougainvillea and orchids and enchanting water features add immeasurably to the ambience of the hotel.

In 1981, a new phase of planting and design was carried out by Michael White, his associate Ketut Marsa and a large team of gardeners. Stone carvings and other objects by Bali's renowned sculptors were added to complement the brilliant display of tropical abundance. Plants were grouped in masses of similar species to create interesting patterns. This concept of lush landscaping was further reinforced by the establishment of the Tropical Horticultural Garden of decorative plants in 1983 which houses the hotel's amazing collection of tropical plants. Many of these plants were initially brought from Singapore and Hawaii and cultivated here before being introduced throughout the gardens of Bali.

One of the intriguing pieces of sculpture found lurking among the thick foliage of Bali Hyatt.

Goa Gajah - This cave in Bali, also known as the Elephant's Cave, is adorned with a monstrous head above its entrance. It appears to have been used to worship the God Shiva.

Landscaped pool deck at Bali Hyatt. A replica of Goa Gajah cave is adapted and used as a waterfall entrance to a man-made cave.
Right: The spectacular gardens of Bali Hyatt are sensitively designed oases full of surprises. Exotic flower beds complement bright tropical blooms.

At Amanpuri, a grand visual
symphony is created through the
compelling landscape.

Hard landscape plays an equally important role as soft landscape at Amanpuri.

Warm timber uprights and balustrades are enhanced by colourful blooms to create an environment of serenity and charm.

Botanical bounty flourish in the tropics.

Colourful "heliconias" are commonly cultivated.

Tanjong Jara Beach Hotel - The picturesque landscape creates a verdant beauty of immense vitality.

Rantau Abang Visitor's Centre is designed around a natural lagoon, which contributes immensely to the general feeling of repose. It possess a refreshing directness and pervasive sensuality that engage the senses.

Water Features

"There is a lady called water.

We can't live without her.

Water is romantic, sensual,

beautiful, happy, strong, sweet,

and fresh. Peace and movement,

limited and eternal, landscape

and architecture, water is life."

— Ricardo Legorreta

An essential component of the landscape at Tanjong Jara Beach Hotel, water receives prominent treatment as an experiential and reflective element.

A bridge over the lagoon at Tanjong Jara.

Water, the ancestral cradle and the primordial sustenance of all life forms, plays an important role in the traditional architecture and city planning of many countries in Southeast Asia. An essential component of the landscape, it receives prominent treatment in gardens as an experiential and reflective element.

From the bubbling fountain to the still pool, water offers spiritual rejuvenation and irresistible appeal. Certainly, it has a magnetising effect more powerful than any other features in the landscape. In the Orient, the use of water goes beyond the merely functional. Since time immemorial, it has been a source of aesthetic pleasure and therapeutic value. Pleasurable outdoor spaces are incomplete without water, whose primary role is to evoke a heightened awareness of nature. In the Islamic gardens, the designers always treat springs and fountains as key architectonic elements. These water features are objects of reverence that interweave between the external and internal spaces, providing spatial continuity as well as creating a visually captivating environment.

Water also plays a symbolic role in Southeast Asia. Few regions in the world possess so many water symbols and water festivals. Historically, water was important for the irrigated cultivation of rice. The local subsistence economy has always been based on wet rice cultivation.

Rantau Abang is sandwiched between the coastal road and the sea. It highlights one of the aspirations of a true work of architecture - the preservation, if not enhancement, of the environment.

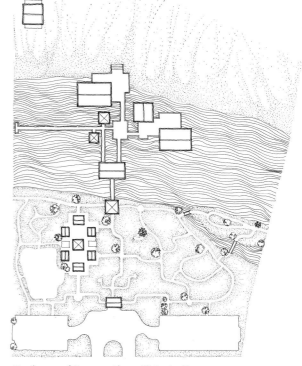

Site layout of Rantau Abang Visitor's Centre, showing its relationship to the water.

Picturesquely composed pools at Amankila Resort (Sanskrit term for peaceful mountain), Bali, are crafted into a sanctuary of calm.

The landscaped 'moats' of Amankila are important design elements.

In Thailand, native art and architecture are full of images of aquatic origins. Water gods are still worshipped today in many parts of Thailand. Many festivals, such as Songkran, the traditional Thai New Year, are associated with rain propitiation. Songkran lasts about 15 days, and the norm is to drench everyone with water for good luck. As a rule, Buddhist monasteries are designed to face a body of water. This is probably derived from the belief that Prince Siddhartha attained enlightenment to become Buddha while meditating under the *Bodhi* tree facing a river.

The use of water was also manifested in the layout of ancient cities and palaces. The presence of water was of paramount importance for the definition of the urban image. There was a perfect functional and aesthetic symbiosis between water and city. At times, entire cities also took on an amphibious nature. Sukhothai, the ancient capital of Thailand, consisted of impressive water-bound temples. These temples were designed with elaborate water features, ponds and lakes either for use as reflecting pools or for ritual bathing. An-

other example was the city of Ayutthaya, which was probably one of the most beautiful and ingeniously planned of Thai ancient cities. Referred to as the "Venice of the East", it was built to resemble an island by the excavation of a 3.5 km long moat around it.

Complex hydraulic engineering, consisting of gravity-fed network of canals and moats, was extensively employed in Khmer classical town planning in the form of diked basins or "baray" which represented the cosmic ocean.

In the Hindu-Buddhist cosmology, Southeast Asia is the habitat of the *naga*, a mythical serpent with magical powers which is well-represented in local folklore and is to be found carved in all forms in buildings as well as daily objects. This aquatic symbol originated as a dragon-shaped cloud over Mahameru, the cosmological centre of the continents. The god Indra slew the cloud to release water which created the

Water features surround every pavilion suite at Amandari.

The natural hues of the lush green Balinese foliage is reflected in the green tiles of the saline pool at Amandari.

Enclosed by luxuriant foliage and high walls, these individual villas at Bali Imperial have their own swimming pools and landscaped water features.

The entrance to a man-made cave at the Bali Hyatt's swimming pool is adorned with an interesting stone carving.

One of the many Balinese stone carvings and water features found in the compound of Wantilan Lama, Batujimbar Estates, Bali.

The beautifully landscaped water features at Bali Imperial are conceived by Bill Bensley Design Group International.

At Grand Hyatt Bali, water features provide an animated effect, offering a delightful visual and aural experience.

One of the many pools at Grand Hyatt Bali.

A stone carving of a Balinese mythological creature is used as a water spout.

rivers and the seas. The *naga* is thus seen as a symbol of the source of life. Its association with water, rain and the rainbow makes it an important and pervasive symbol in Southeast Asia's cultural heritage. In Thailand, the *naga* can be found on wall murals, water jars and temple roofs. The multiple roof edges and gable-boards of ordination halls in temples are usually framed with the sinuous bodies and multipleflared heads of the *naga*.

Many landscaped gardens are interwoven with a series of awe-inspiring ponds filled with pink and white lotus. The most vivid images of such magnificent water-laced gardens are to be found in the courtyard compounds of the Balinese house and the traditional royal palace, the "Puri Agung". They can also be found in elaborate Javanese royal pleasure grounds. These water-borne palaces are usually surrounded by mirror-like reflecting pools filled with lotus, water-lily, water hyacinth and water lettuce. Of the surviving examples, the Taman Sari water palace of Yogyakarta, also known as the Water Castle (or Kraton Hamengkubuwono) is probably the grandest. There is an extensive network of canals, ponds, fountains and bathing pools. Such landscaped ponds form an integral part of the architecture. They are used to create a feeling of repose. The magical quality is further enhanced by the dappled play of ever-changing light off the water.

With the increasing consciousness among the public of the importance of landscape design in the tropics, water as a design element takes on more varied forms.

Guests at Club Med Bali are greeted by cascading streams and landscaped pools.

The pool at Sheraton Senggigi Beach Resort is the main focal point. A variegated grey and reddish slate ("batu tembel") was used for the pool sides and landscaped paths, while a green slate ("batu sukabumi") was used to line the pool gutters.

Pools for recreational purposes are designed to enhance the architecture and the immediate surroundings. They are usually incorporated into garden designs, especially those in resort hotels. Many are either softened by dense planting along the edges or are designed in various imaginative freeform configurations.

Most contemporary resorts are designed with extensive water features because of their unique attributes of reflecting light. A most notable example is the contoured swimming pool at Amandari Resort in Bali, where the seemingly floating pool of water reflects the colour of the rice terraces on the hill slopes through the use of coloured mosaic tiles. This is a wonderful example of natural phenomena been given increased presence through the use of colour and water.

There is an increasing respect for the use of water in a naturalistic context. Cascading streams and landscaped pools found in many hotels are carefully designed to evoke an uncontrived effect. At the Bali Hyatt's swimming pool, for example, Bill Bensley has designed a replica of the famous rock carving of Goa Gajah to serve as a mini-waterfall.

For the Sheraton Senggigi Beach Resort in Lombok, the island east of Bali, Bensley has created a fantasy pool set among lush gardens. The focus of the pool is an enormous stone head, modelled after a traditional Sasak art form, which conceals a water slide. These features provide ample evidence that water has many distinguishing qualities and can be the most attractive and compelling element when carefully designed.

Carvings of turtles serve as stools in the swim-up bar.

The "Kepala Besar" is an enormous stone head made of Javanese andesite and modelled after a traditional Sasak art form. It conceals a water slide.

Delightful stone carvings are littered all over the resort. Whimsy and delight are the principles which guided the design of the entire project.

The pool at The Beaufort, Singapore, lined with iridescent blue-black tiles, has a sense of dense quietude. It is set on a cliff which overlooks the beach below.

The open spaces between the buildings are filled with water gardens.

View of the pool in the Precima House, Malaysia, which extends into the living space.

The pool in the Precima House is set amid congenial and contemplative surroundings.

An internal landscaped pool in the Lee Residence, Singapore, assists in amplifying the melodious sound of falling water.
Overleaf: The pervasive presence of water in this house at Belmont Road, Singapore, designed by Ernesto Bedmar, produces an emotional effect of profound serenity.

Edged by the azure sea of Pansea Bay and topped by the unwavening blue sky, Amanpuri is conceived with water as a key element.

A spacious pool in one of the private villas at Amanpuri.

The unruffled calm of the centrally located black-tiled swimming pool in Amanpuri, measuring 23m x 8m, is a visual complement to the crystalline Andaman Sea.

Water has been a dominant feature of life in Thailand's history. These traditional structures evolved along the banks of canals and waterways.

A traditional Thai monastery library ("haw-trai") stands in a lily pond. Many traditional buildings have an amphibious character because of their close relationships to water.

This elaborate water feature forms the focal point in the gardens of the Sanphet Prasat Palace in Muang Boran, Thailand.

The entrance court of Club Med Bali demonstrates a logic of scale and proportion with admirable ease.

Courtyards

"It is beautiful when we limit

space. When we create a patio,

we become owners of that space.

Before, it belonged to everybody;

after, it is ours. Patios are

romantic, intimate; they give

us a sense of property and

security. Light, colour, and

water are enhanced there."

- Ricardo Legorreta

The courtyard is a recurring theme of the built environment in many diverse cultures. As a symbolic generic form, it consists of many varieties of physical realisation. Its existence throughout history in diverse geographical belts is an indication of its great viability. From the covered courtyards with clerestory windows in Morocco to the underground courtyards of the Gobi deserts to the Chinese courtyard dwellings, secluded courtyards are central to the hierarchical nature of spatial organisation. They are conceived as private realms for contemplation and dreams, an arcadian vision where man can make peace with himself.

The word "paradise" is derived from the old Persian word 'pairidaeza', which means enclosed garden. Courtyards thus have the singular objective of defining space where nature and artifice meet. These "rooms without roofs" are microcosms that are mini-representations of nature and the cosmos. They are enchanting not just because they contain greenery but because they possess an undeniable ambience of quietude and completeness. Besides foliage, man's physical and spiritual needs are also cultivated in courtyards.

This sense of containment can be achieved through several typologies. The most common is the closed court, located in the centre of the building mass. It is an ancient dwelling form that has been appreciated by the early civilisations of Mesopotamia, Egypt, Greece, Rome and China. The tranquil area is designed for privacy, recreation and work. All rooms face a courtyard on the ground level open to the sky. The through court is one variation in which a passage links the court with the exteriors. A third type is the corner court, often expressed as a walled garden. Another common variation is the implied courtyard, loosely defined by landscape elements or adjacent buildings that delimit the contained positive space.

An intimate courtyard at Bali Oberoi.

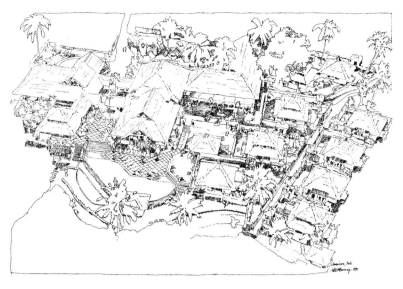

Each pavilion suite at Amandari has private courtyards
enclosed by high walls.
Right: Aerial view of Amandari showing the many private
and semi-private courtyards.

One of the two duplex pavilion suites with its own private pool in the garden courtyard.

As a special symbol of introversion, the light and airy courtyard is a wonderful device, not just in the way its micro climate enhances living conditions but also for how sensitively and fully it serves the occupants. This "open-to-sky" space brings light, rain, natural draught and a feeling of openness into the interiors, modulating the spatial effects of the rooms as well as renewing essential contact with the organic world. At the same time, it serves as a reference space where all other ancillary areas are related to it physically.

The courtyard is predominant in the indigenous urban settlements of Southeast Asia. It is efficient in the utilisation of land and provides a private outdoor space even in areas of high density housing. Houses are built around courtyards, open to the sky, yet secluded from neighbouring lots and from the crowded streets by high enclosing walls. The urban architectural tradition of Singapore and Malaysia is characterised by the traditional shop-house. These long narrow buildings have central air wells that provide light and ventilation. Exhibiting eclectic mixes of Chinese, Malay, Renaissance, English and Dutch influences, the shophouse type forms the basic component of the urban fabric in these two countries.

Interestingly, the entrance of most courtyard dwellings is almost inevitably characterised by a non-axial form of entry, created by an intrinsic visual privacy feature – the "spirit wall". Crossing the threshold of a gateway, one has to turn at right angles to enter the internal courtyard from the public domain. Evil spirits are supposedly unable to enter since they cannot negotiate corners, being able to travel only in straight lines.

The progression from a public space to a semi-private realm prevents any overlooking in a courtyard. For example, in the Buddhist temple compound of Thailand, an outer and inner wall separates the temple grounds from secular areas with the

A verdant sun-drenched courtyard in Russell Whitechurch's Residence, Bali. Traditional qualities are reinstated in this serene space.

Courtyards in Balinese aristocratic dwellings are filled with individual pavilions used for different functions. The entire complex is made up of an introspective labyrinth of interconnecting courtyards and pavilions.

This courtyard in Ubud, Bali, consists of a narrow, moat-like pond and a stone bridge set amid lush foliage. It was clearly inspired by the water gardens that were an important feature in traditional palaces.

inner wall usually taking the form of cloister-like galleries filled with Buddha images. Moving through the gate across a high threshold, one is immediately transported into a private sanctum perceivably different from the public world.

The layout of a typical Balinese enclosed courtyard is composed in a similar manner. In an aristocratic dwelling, the whole complex is actually made up of an introspective labyrinth of inter-connecting courtyards and pavilions. Gateways are sometimes characterised by split gates, with the "spirit wall" immediately behind it.

The simplest form of gateway is the *angkul-angkul*, an entrance portal with two pillars holding up a thatched roof. The gateway is usually built of *paras*, a kind of volcanic sand stone or bricks. But the location of open-air structures within the courtyard is spatially determined by a cosmological diagram that represents an ideal order. There are theoretically eight cardinal points and a central point. The latter is simply an open space for general family activities while the family temple is always located in the north-eastern corner. The *bale gede*, a square pavilion on a high base located in the east, serves as the space for family ceremonies, whereas the western pavilion, *bale dauh*, is the children's sleeping area.

Most Balinese temples consists of two courtyards, the outer and inner courts. Entry to the forecourt is characterised by the imposing presence of *candi bentar*, the split gate, which is like the two halves of a solid structure that has been sliced through the centre and pushed apart. The two inner sides are usually smooth, in contrast to the ornate outer sides. Entry to the inner court is again through another monumental and elaborately carved gate known as the *padu raksa*. It resembles the re-combined halves of the *candi bentar* but is always elevated on stone platform. A flight of stone steps on each side leads up to the narrow doorway that carries an image of the god Boma.

Monumental gateways open into the inner courtyards of traditional Balinese temples.

Courtyards of Balinese temples are richly articulated spaces.

Pergolas cast delightful patterns on the pool's surface in one of the many semi-enclosed courtyards at Amanusa, Bali.

At the Four Seasons Resort, intimate courtyards contribute immeasurably to the ambience of the place.

A traditional Balinese pavilion, the "bale", serves as a sitting area in the courtyard of a private villa at Bali Imperial.

Pebbled courtyard between the main block and the service block of the Reuter House, Singapore.

In traditional Javanese palaces, a large central courtyard represents the sacred mountain, Mahameru. This quiet courtyard is always connected in a symmetrical manner to a series of walls, high gateways and smaller courtyards arranged in a north-south axis. Symbolically, the gates and courtyards represent a complex series of concentric rings of continents and seas respectively. Marvellous examples of traditional Javanese court architecture can be found in the old city of Yogyakarta (traditionally known as Mataram). The *keraton* or palace symbolises the model of the Javanese cosmos. Similar cosmological models were used in palace architecture in many other places like Solo and Cirebon. The definite sequence of ritualistic spaces in these buildings demonstrates that in Hindu-Javanese architecture, each courtyard space is incomplete unless it is integrated into the entire complex.

There is no doubt that courtyard spaces heighten the quality of the environment. The benefits to the occupants can be expressed in physical, environmental, psychological and social terms. They yield many lessons in the handling of open spaces and transitions. It is for these reasons that they provide profound architectural experiences, and evoke a primary response in our subconsciousness.

A typical airwell in a traditional shophouse of Peninsular Malaysia. These airwells, often paved in 'Melaka tile', a derivative of Dutch Delft tiles, bring light and ventilation to this unique component of the urban fabric of all Malaysian cities.

Two sunken, black-tiled pools form the focus of this internal courtyard in the Lee Residence, Belmont Road, Singapore. On the second storey, a bridge across the atrium links the family space to the bedrooms.

Heintji Moo's Residence, Singapore.
Top: Views into the central courtyard.
Above: The courtyard, opened to the sky, is surrounded by the living-dining-kitchen areas.

The heart of the house, designed by Juan Peck Foon, is the pebbled 20 sq m courtyard. Light is the ineffable presence, contributing to the different moods of the house at different times of the day.

Narrow courtyards in a traditional Thai structure.

Traditional Thai dwellings have open courtyards surrounded by different pavilions. These spaces are used for ceremonies, feasting, drying food and gardening.

A large pavilion in a house at Batujimbar, Bali. The absence of walls provide an intimate sense of the outdoors.

In-Between Realms

Architecture should be conceived

of as a configuration of inter-

mediary places clearly defined...

it implies a break away from

the contemporary concept...

of spatial continuity and

the tendency to erase every

articulation between spaces.

- Aldo van Eyck

One of the most important spaces in all buildings in the tropics is surely the transition zone. Although the primary function of a building is shelter, its richness is derived from the simultaneous experience of the interior and the exterior. This "in-between realm" – the amorphous and ambiguous edge between inside and out, private and public, hot and cold, security and vulnerability, shadow and light – has always been a crucial element in the vocabulary of spatial forms.

One person who has thought deeply about this in-between space is Dutch architect Aldo van Eyck. He has asserted that "Architecture should be conceived of as a configuration of intermediary places clearly defined... it implies a break away from the contemporary concept... of spatial continuity and the tendency to erase every articulation between spaces, i.e. between outside and inside, between one space and another... Instead the transition must be articulated by means of defined in-between places which induce simultaneous awareness of what is significant on either sides. An in-between space in this sense provides a common ground where conflicting polarities can again become twin phenomena."

Yet strangely, this interesting category of architectural space has not received systematic analyses by academicians and has been the subject of neglect by many architects. Rigorous understanding of this realm can provide many lessons in the best

The sheltered space in this bale is neither inside nor outside, but belongs equally to both the internal and the external worlds.

The archetype of Balinese construction, the bale, exemplifies the in-between realm.

In this contemporary Balinese structure, terraces extend into the interior
while overhanging roofs extend out into the gardens.

means for dealing with the climate. This sheltered space is neither outside nor inside, but belongs equally to both the internal and the external worlds. There is no clear demarcation in terms of boundary lines. The edges between grounds and buildings are left undefined as pavements, gardens, and even pools extend into and even through the building while overhanging roofs and cantilevered structures extend out into the surroundings. Weaving spaces flow and overlap, and interpenetrate each other, evoking vibrations of a deep psychological nature.

The in-between realm is a vital and essential link between architecture and the landscape, maximising the interface between the inside and the natural surroundings. In a temperate climate, architects tend to maximise the solidity of the external walls (hence the wall becomes an essential element of built form), sharply differentiating between the inside and out. This is not the case in the tropics, where built forms possess a continuum of spaces leading from the interior to the exterior. Many Southeast Asian societies exhibit ambiguous relationships between figure and ground, built form and external space.

The delightful indeterminate zone of the in-between realm is intrinsic to the tropical consciousness. Generally, transition spaces include a variety of modalities – loggia, verandah, balcony, patio, terrace, colonnade, pergola, pavilion, passageway and external staircase. As architectural elements, they have been constructed with varying degrees of protection in an almost

Covered walkways at Club Med Bali.
Preceding page: Landscaped pool in a palatial private compound at Batujimbar, Bali, seen from one of the many in-between spaces around it.

The main lobby area at Grand Hyatt Bali is orientated to take full advantage of the prevailing breezes. These pleasant spaces allow the guests to experience and enjoy the ineffably changing presence of the natural elements.

At the Four Seasons Resort in Bali, a sense of simplicity is achieved by spaces that interweave between the outside and the inside.

Definition between the interior and the exterior becomes blurred in these walkways.

The in-between spaces at Amandari are vital links between the architecture and the landscape, maximising the interface between the inside and the outside.

infinite variety of forms and spatial configuration, from the traditional open-walled pavilion of Balinese architecture, the *bale*, to the verandah or *serambi* of the traditional Malay dwelling, to the *sala* (a roofed pavilion without walls) of Thai architecture. This *sala* is essentially a raised timber platform with a gabled roof supported by columns. Building one is seen as an act of merit and they are thus found throughout Thailand. The Sasaks of Lombok in Indonesia also spend most of their time outside the house in open-walled structures.

Complementing the enclosed interiors of many buildings are other elements like balconies and verandahs. The former are essentially either projections from a building or recessed into it, serving as semi-outdoor spaces. Usually situated above the ground, they extend the flow of interior space into the surroundings. Verandahs are exceptionally practical devices that also serve as outdoor rooms and provide a sense of shelter as well as a physical shelter from the heat and torrential downpour and at the same time, allowing the occupants to experience the ineffably changing presence of the natural elements. Buildings also derive much appeal from the interesting pattern of light and shadow that is created by these elements. The form of verandah introduced by the British builders in Southeast Asia was actually indigenous to the medieval vernacular architecture of Spain and Portugal. It was transported to Brazil where the British later

Verandahs at Club Med Cherating, Malaysia, serve as outdoor rooms.

Long circulation routes at Club Med Cherating are treated as important architectural elements and delightful transition spaces.

adapted it for the climatic conditions of India and Southeast Asia.

Circulation elements can also form one of the most interesting transition spaces. They are a potential source of vitality in any building. Routes joining different buildings or through a building can be treated as an essential experience, fundamental to comprehending its form and providing a sense of the outdoors. The building and its relation to the site gains a further experiential coherence.

In-between spaces are undeniably essential elements of Southeast Asian built form. The distinctive feature about them is that though functionally they are unspecific, they can fulfil a variety of activities. These pleasant and inviting spaces are very versatile, providing a simple shelter for the occupants to entertain, dine, relax and enjoy the scenery. Sensitive designers have shown in their works a conscious awareness of the importance of these spaces and have intelligently re-worked and cultivated traditional solutions into their buildings, thereby recovering those qualities which are lost in the vacuous functionalism of the recent past.

The delightful indeterminate zone of the in-between realm includes a variety of balconies and terraces, as seen in Pelangi Beach Resort, Malaysia.

Proportioned and detailed with a minimalist rigour, the corridor spaces of The Beaufort, Singapore, are richly nuanced through the interplay of shifting light.

The corridor spaces at night.

House in Bin Tong Park. The outdoor room extends the flow of interior space into carefully landscaped gardens.

The high-pitched roof and sheltering eaves are the house's most salient features.

Deep overhangs provide physical shelter from the heat and torrential downpour.

Non-airconditioned public spaces do not require enclosing walls to keep out the rain and heat, as seen in Amanpuri.

The spatial fluidity of the reception lobby at Amanpuri achieves careful gradations as the continuum of spaces leads from the interior to the exterior.

The absence of enclosing walls at Amanpuri maximises the interface between the inside and the landscape.

The interplay between the storey-height glass doors and the timber column is reminiscent of traditional architecture. An intimate relationship between outdoors and indoors is thus achieved in this private villa in Amanpuri.

The open-sided roofed pavilion or "sala" an Amanpuri serves as a rest area. "Sala" comes from the Sanskrit term of the same name, which means "an ascetic's hermitage".

Steeply-pitched roofs that almost touch the ground in this Thai structure make walls unnecessary.

Spaces beneath traditional Thai buildings raised on stilts provide crucial links with the outdoors.

Transition spaces in a traditional Thai house derive much appeal from the interesting patterns of light and shadow.

In-between spaces are undeniably essential elements of Southeast Asian built form.

Landscape architect Michael White's house in Sayan, Bali. Located above the dramatic Ayung Gorge, the openings are designed to maximise views of the spectacular surroundings. The Sayan ridge is host to artistic itinerants from all over the world.

Openings

"*Every door is at once a*

boundary, shutting off one

area from another, and also

a bond between the inside

and the outside."

- Gretl Hoffmann

Aman Brioche, Sayan, Bali.

The Austrian novelist Herman Broch once said that we may comprehend the essence of an era from its architectural facades. The forms of doors, windows and other openings that penetrate the solid planes of walls are countless. This rich vocabulary of important architectural features may vary from the rustic to the elaborate, and the modest to the imposing. To encourage maximum amount of cross ventilation in the tropics, buildings usually have a large number of huge openings.

An opening can be located within a wall, the ceiling or between two planes. Openings have always been focal points of a building's elevation. They are important in shaping our perception of built form and this endows them crucial roles in the use of the buildings.

Although they have different design functions, doors and windows are conceptually similar. They serve functionally to link spaces and channel the direction of movement. A simple opening like a door in an external wall physically connects the enclosure to the surroundings. The occupants are kept in tune with the perpetual variations of the earth and sky. But doors are more than merely holes of entrance and exit. Symbolically, they are significant because they represent the exposed threshold between the private domain and the public realm.

Over the centuries, Southeast Asian craftsmen have incorporated allegorical implications and the physical functions of doors and windows into a coherent iconographic programme. The traditional Thai and Balinese doors have been one of the region's most elaborately carved architectural elements, serving to illustrate the infinite possibilities of wood-carving. The door and window frames of traditional Thai architecture are constructed as trap-

Fenestration treatment at Aman Brioche.

The openings in this villa in Sayan, Bali, display a conscious striving for simplicity.

Exquisitely carved door in a private compound in Sanur, Bali.

An interesting doorway at the entrance to one of the private villas at Bali Imperial.

A traditional Balinese door serves as a side entrance into one of the pavilions at Taman Mertasari, Sanur.

Detail of an opening in the walls of Club Med Bali.

ezoids, with the base tapering towards the top. Painted Thai doors and panels usually depict guardian figures interwoven with symbolic motifs. Each door consists of a pair of leaves set in a timber frame which rests directly on the threshold. Depending on the various eras, the main subjects of the door leaves could be guardian divinities with swords or diminutive creatures in a forest setting.

Gilding, the practice of applying gold leaf as a decorative device, is a common feature on the doors and windows in Thailand. The lacquered panels may also be embellished with mythical scenes rendered in intricate mother-of-pearl inlays. The frames, whether in stone or carved in wood, are also highly ornamented with gilded motifs or engraved with decorative and symbolic animals of auspicious nature. They usually represent mythical ideas regarding entrance. Some are crowned by elaborate pediments depicting peacocks or *nagas*. Besides creating a visual stimulus, the finely sculpted doorway raises the simple act of crossing a threshold to a ceremonial event. Daily life is not banalised, but is instead exalted to become rich and meaningful.

Windows act as filters in the building's envelope, bringing light and air into the interiors. By their degree of closure, interiors can become bright and airy, or cool and reclusive. They provide views, thereby

Handsomely proportioned doors lined up in an axial manner.

Elaborately carved and refined details are characteristic of traditional Balinese doors.

Two guardian figures flank an elaborate entrance gate to a private compound in Sanur, Bali.

A gateway elevated on steps leads into the inner sanctum of a Balinese aristocratic dwelling.

Different types of Balinese entrance gates. Built of either local volcanic sandstone or corals, they are objects of elemental vigour.

Detail of full-length windows designed in the manner of traditional Malay architecture.

bringing the landscape and foliage into focus. In Chinese garden design, various shaped openings are cut into the walls to act as picture frames, emphasising a part of a well-composed setting for contemplative purposes. Other kinds of openings reveal, at least partially, of what lies beyond, acting as a magnet to draw one forward.

The word "window" is actually derived from the old Norse word for "wind", combined with the word for "eye". Thus it literally means an "eye" of a building through which the wind flows. Windows primarily serve the vital function of illuminating and ventilating the interior space. Their many functions may be in conflict with one another. For example, although they provide light and air, they also allow heat gain and noise transmission. The quality of light in the interiors, whether direct or diffused, soft or harsh, is also affected by the size and placement of openings. In the tropics, glare from the skies and ground reflections is a major problem and openings need to be shaded to reduce direct solar gain and glare.

In the traditional Malay house, the windows are often full-length and are fully operable, extending all the way down to the floor level. Decorated with elaborate engravings, the panels are divided into three sections of which the top piece is usually a fixed panel. Many have adjustable louvres or shutters which allow ventilation even when the windows are closed. The windows in the domestic buildings of Thai-

The traditional Malay house's windows, though simple, are sensitively designed. They are usually full-length and divided into three sections, some with adjustable louvres.

Window treatment of the chalet at Pelangi, Malaysia, follows the traditional style.

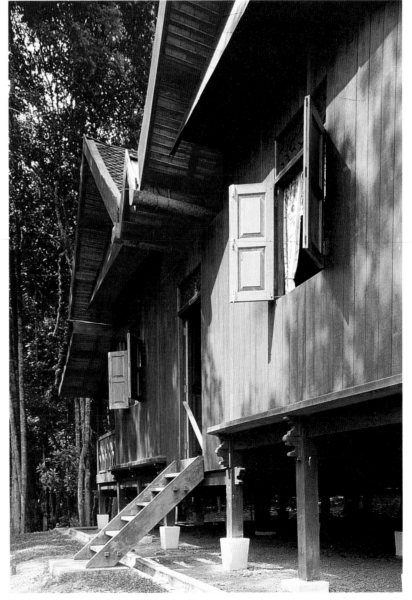

Window treatment in a typical Malay house.

land and Myanmar (Burma), and among the Acehnese and Bugis of Indonesia, also extend to the floor level. Such well-designed openings offer privacy, security and comfort as well as aesthetic appeal.

While the importance of openings cannot be overlooked, developments in the 20th century constructional techniques and aesthetic principles have fundamentally changed the traditional perceptions and concepts of doors and windows. Today, the design of openings is a source of endless variety in materials and colours. Glass openings as an architectural element are now being used throughout buildings in the region. Recent developments like sliding glass panes offer important expressive potential. They help to protect the interiors from the elements as well as provide an unimpeded view. Through such extensive use of glass doors, man's need of relating himself to nature is easily realised. Modern technology also offers a wide range of glass for the designer. The task of creating an appropriate treatment for openings in contemporary buildings of Southeast Asia is at once exciting and demanding. Possibilities may have changed but the relationships between walls and doors or windows remain significant. The quest for expressive relationships between solid and void continues.

Reuter House. Contemporary interpretation of the British colonial bungalow in Singapore.

Glass windows and a centrally pivoted door allow fabulous views of the garden in this house in Cluny Road, Singapore.

Projecting eaves of a pavilion suite at Amanpuri protect the doors and windows from heavy tropical downpours.

A pair of sliding doors in one of Amanpuri's private villas.

The entire length of the living unit's walls consists of full-height glazing.

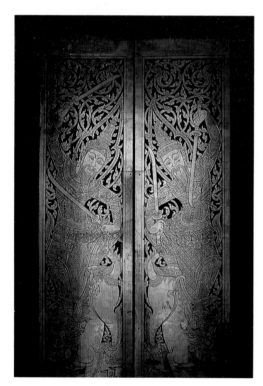
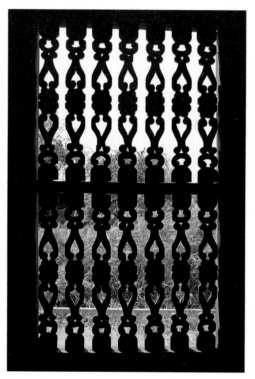

Traditional Thai doors and openings have been one of the region's most elaborately carved architectural elements.

The often-employed method of having the walls and windows in Thai architecture tapering slightly towards the top.

Gilded windows in a traditional Thai structure in Bangkok.

Windows in the Jim Thompson House, Bangkok.

This traditional Thai house, the Ho Kham, built during the Ratanakosin period, is elevated high on stilts. Its elaborately carved windows are the most distinctive feature on the elevations.

The living room of the Thompson House, Bangkok. Silk fabrics and Thai antiques add a vivid splash of colour to the teak background.

Interiors and Details

"A plan proceeds from within to
without. A building is like a soap
bubble. This bubble is perfect and
harmonious if the breath has been
evenly distributed and regulated
from the inside. The exterior is
the result of an interior."

- Le Corbusier

The exterior of a building is the result of various factors and influences. In some cases, it conveys an image of the owner which he wishes to project to the public. But the interior, especially in a family dwelling, always reveals more of the owner's taste, self perception and lifestyle through the choice of adornment and decoration. According to architectural historian Norberg-Schulz, "... it offers him a refuge where he can feel at home and be at peace with himself, and it serves as a starting-point for his actions in the world." He further adds: "The interior of a house is different from that of other buildings. A house is used by a small group of people and its character is both personal and private. It is the result of a deliberate choice."

Among the interiors featured, some similar characteristics can be discerned. What is evident is an expression of a unique lifestyle through a mix of thoughtful space planning and clean, uncluttered detailing.

These are spaces that are wonderful to live in because they are well organised and also because they harmonise with the external architectural treatment. All are commited to designs executed in an unpretentious style, deploying indigenous materials and decorative motifs with sensitivity and authority. They are also usually the effort of the same eloquent architect who has shaped the structures, thus ensuring that the details only serve to emphasise the architecture's generating principles. It is difficult for interior designers who are not involved at the start of a project to penetrate into the architect's philosophy and intention. Consequently, such contrived interiors often lack depth and conviction, and are ultimately incompatible with the architecture.

In the field of resort design, architects are taking up the challenge of designing interiors that reconcile the contradictory needs for luxury and simplicity, sophistication and serenity. The solutions are usu-

The interior of the Thompson House is filled with extensive collections of Asian art.

Seated sandstone Buddha in Lopburi-Khmer style, 13th century. The ubiquitous Buddha image is a reminder of the Buddhist doctrine in human form.

Some of the exquisite Asian art collections found in the living room of the Thompson House.

View of the bedroom suite in a private villa at Amanpuri.

ally historically inspired, yet contemporary in their response to the guests' needs. These effects work together to create interiors that evoke the intrinsic sensuality of the architecture. A palette of traditional materials are carefully selected and deftly deployed. There is a continuity of interest as vistas open and close. They also provide a setting for a panoply of Southeast Asian art. The blend of traditional and modern furnishings as well as the textual differentiation of materials make the rooms a haven of relaxation.

The individuality of a building is also very much the result of its details. It is the individual detail that arrests our attention. The sense of the whole is comprehended through the sense of its parts. There exists in Southeast Asia a long tradition of architectural philosophy which sees the relation between whole and part as crucial to the beauty of a building.

Details crafted to exacting standards can provide foci of interest which visually enliven the building, adding greatly to the enjoyment of the architecture and putting *joie de vivre* back into contemporary experience. These details also enhance the occupants' lives by resolving functional problems and uniting the interior with the exterior in a seamless manner.

The refined proportions of many traditional details create an undoubted visual allure. There is a wealth of traditional architectural solutions which can be incorporated in the modern context. Many architects are now evoking vernacular solutions to practical problems. Such quoting of established sources is made on the basis of visual impact, quality and appro-

The spartan quality of the interiors evokes a simple elegance.

Cotton fabrics used for the cushions, bed-covers and pillows are woven in Bangkok. A carved "chofa" flanks the double bed.

Traditional Thai artefacts employed as decorative features in an interior space.

Left and above: Living area in one of Amanpuri's private villas. Subtle but controlled lighting at each of the columns adds to the overall calm ambience. Overleaf: Monochromatic interior finishes in Amanpuri's reading room are made of local materials. All the veneer for the columns, mouldings and framing is of "maka", a local hardwood.

The Sukhothai Hotel in Bangkok is a blend of rustic simplicity and blissful serenity.

priateness. These beautifully executed details are skilfully juxtaposed with contemporary methods of construction, all of which are fittingly deployed within the framework of a governing concept. The success of some of the finest detailing is also due to the designer's elimination of extraneous elements. Dutch architect Aldo van Eyck once defined a good building as "... one that has what it should have and hasn't got what it needn't have."

Collections of traditional art and fine antiques are complementary to the Southeast Asian interior setting. Southeast Asian sculpture is now beginning to achieve the worldwide appreciation it deserves, with many scholars acknowledging that the region's sculptures are on par with that of Egypt and Greece in terms of artistic accomplishment.

The ubiquitous Buddha image in Thailand, Burma and Cambodia, for example, lends an air of contemplative grace to any space. Buddha images, depicted as seated, standing, reclining or walking, are carved out of stone or cast in bronze, ranging in size from a few centimetres to several metres. These images are always depicted with the hands placed in gestures or "mudras" signifying various events in Buddha's life. Their iconographic forms, however, are interpreted in an exclusively religious manner. Like most Southeast Asian works of art, the aesthetic judgment is not based on external appearance alone.

Wooden carvings made of the best types of hardwood such as *chengal* or *kempas* are also commonly used as architectural features. In traditional Malay wood carving, the decorative motif composition found on eaves, barge-boards, architraves, railings and wall panels are guided by rules inherited by ethnic groups such as the Minangkabaus, Bugis, Javanese and Achehnese.

Close-up of ornamental wall feature in The Beaufort, Singapore.

Interior of one of the villas at The Beaufort.

In Amandari's suites, the furniture and fabrics are designed with great restraint by Neville Marsh.

Southeast Asia also enjoys a reputation as a veritable paradise for the range of its unique applied arts, which are closely bounded to the religious and domestic needs of the people. Handcrafted objects of incomparable grace are produced in an amazing array of texture and colours. They provide fascinating examples of a love for beauty and functional inventiveness.

Most of these painstakingly crafted artefacts are created in small cottage industries, employing time-honoured traditional skills passed down from generation to generation. These artisans have incorporated design features from the rich artistic traditions of both India and China into the ethnic peculiarities of their folk-craft. In the words of art critic Philip Rawson, "The best of this art combines a sensuous sweetness with a luxuriant magnificence, blending joy and delight with intense intellectual and imaginative strength. The sweetness may occasionally veer towards the febrile, the strength towards crudity.

But the virtue of each art is always its own. Each can offer us an imaginative experience which must extend our mental horizons."

There is great demand for these exquisite goods that include ceramics, rattan products, furniture, traditional carvings, tribal jewellery, textiles, paintings and ornate silverware. Furniture made in the region is usually from rattan and wicker. In fact, Indonesia has become the prime source of rattan and its product, woven furniture. However, rattan was not used for the construction of furniture until recently and the increasing awareness of the export potential of rattan furniture has led to the development of an active industry.

Other objects like rugs, fabrics, silk, *ikat* textiles and batiks are chosen for their supple texture and durability, but perhaps above all, for their bold designs, fine embroidery and infinite variety of stylised motifs. The shimmering colours and patterns of the magnificent *ikat* textiles of

Amandari's pavilion suites are built from traditional materials painstakingly crafted together.

Bathroom of Villa Bebek splashed in shades of red.

Strong colours enlivened Villa Bebek's interior.

Central Sulawesi are treasured as symbols of wealth and power and commonly used as ceremonial hangings. Originally woven as funeral shrouds; these textiles are now sold as works of art . There are also more than 3000 beautifully patterned batik designs in existence, many with early origins. This textile tradition that reached a high degree of perfection about 200 years ago is a further tribute to the imagination and craftsmanship of the people of Southeast Asia.

The visual allure of many of these objects in domestic settings contribute to the creation of an oasis of well-being. But the survival of some of these crafts hangs in the balance. Fortunately, there has been a resurgence of interest in the values and practices of the craft traditions. National leaders and a vanguard of designers continue to provide substantial patronage and encouragement to the small reservoir of skilled artisans. Southeast Asia surely ranks among the greatest well-springs of artistic achievements and religious intensity. It is hoped that this rich cultural heritage continues to get the recognition and support it deserves.

Interior layout and art objects can combine to create a fully unified expression, thus affirming and heightening the non-reducible experiences of life. Tropical living that is achieved through the imaginative use of outdoor and indoor elements engage our senses, and re-establish architecture's ties with human experiences.

An internal transition space in Villa Bebek.

The master bedroom in House A, Bali, is richly decorated with traditional elements.

An interesting scallop-shaped sunken bathtub rendered in red cement screed in House A.

Bamboo furniture and the visual allure of handwoven objects contribute to the creation of an oasis of well-being.

Southeast Asian artefacts are a tribute to timeless craftsmanship.

The voluminous roof of this house at Belmont Road, designed by Ernesto Bedmar, gives the interior of the living space a high sense of drama.

The interior demonstrates a concern for distilling essentials.

Living room of a Bangkok house designed by Suwan Kongkhunthian, who also designed the water hyacinth sofas to complement the terracotta floor finish.

An indoor pond with an intricate mosaic artwork featuring sun, moon and wave motifs.
Right: Bangkok house by Kongkhunthian. Timber louvred windows of the study room open into an internal airwell.

Bin Tong Park House, Singapore. The "outdoor room" is designed for entertaining guests. Bamboo furniture complements the rustic feel of other materials like exposed timber rafters and terracotta floor tiles.

View of the gallery space. A bar counter is located at the far end of the double-volume space.
Right: Simple, clean lines dominate the interiors. The dining space is visually linked to the living and gallery spaces.

Heintji Moo's Residence, Singapore. Designer Juan prefers to use natural materials like terracotta tiles, teak and nyatoh wood in this open-concept interior.
Right: A minimalist rigour is clearly evident in this interior. A cosy niche is created by turning the corner of the walls into openings.

In creating this interior in a colonial-style bungalow in Singapore, the owners adopted a style they termed as "rustic ethnic." The warm brown and white colour scheme provides an ideal setting for the display of Asian artefacts.

An interior of another colonial-style bungalow in Alexandra Park, Singapore. Built in 1936, there is a spirit of delightful eclecticism. An extraordinary collection of objects provide drama and elegance.

Decorative objects like these Indonesian artefacts play a crucial role in creating a thematic palette for any interior.

De Lange Residence, Singapore. Southeast Asian artefacts lend their share of vitality to the living room.

(Re)Presenting the Vernacular:
(Re)Inventing Authenticity

As mentioned in the *Preface* of the book, the intention here is to showcase the sensitive physicality of tradition-based architecture in Southeast Asia, through photographic essays organised around those recurring architectural features that are strongly manifested in the region. The purpose of any architectural photograph should not merely be to document a building, but to reveal the architect's subtle intents and offer the viewer different ways of perceiving the building. When photographer Berenice Abbott was questioned on the supposedly 'documentary' nature of her oeuvre, her reply was: "There is no such thing as being too objective. Goethe said it — 'Few people have the imagination for reality.' "[1]

This phrase "the imagination for reality" triggers off certain questions which I feel are necessary to be articulated here. The buildings featured in the book are all excellent works. But to what extent have they contributed to the generation of vital forms of regional culture? Or are they simply picturesque scenography — locally crafted Western architecture attempting to communicate a distinct cultural identity and masquerading as "the real thing"?

Architects are all flocking to Bali — to see neither the majestic temple complexes nor the traditional village dwellings — but instead to visit the most recently completed resorts "built in an *authentic* traditional style" for the elite. There is a widespread interest in the quest for more authentic ways to give meanings to new works. These resorts, as well as many private dwellings, are mainly conceived by expatriate architects who all share the same prevailing aim of "re-inventing" authenticity. The much used (or abused) concept of authenticity has been bandied by architects in the developing countries for some time now. It has almost become a panacea for the perceived failure of Modernism. The fact that the past cannot be re-claimed; the programme for these contemporary resorts is a modern invention; and the constructional techniques are part of the phenomenon of universalisation; all these make it a necessity for "authenticity" to be re-invented in these works.

Modern technology (but certainly not Modernism's utopian ideology) is harnessed under a different guise while indigenous archetypes and traditional iconography are appropriated in a controlled manner to create this "authentic" architecture. This claim to "authenticity" is usually substantiated and validated by comparisons with two other categories of buildings — the unashamedly Modernist high-rise structure, or the "fake" regionalist work which is still ostensibly Modernist but uses surface applications of traditional motifs in a gratuitous and eclectic manner that is usually out of context. Ready-made symbols are used in ways totally unrelated to the means of construction.

This admiration for the vernacular results in the perpetuation of an architectural language that assumes the status of authenticity through ensuring a perceived historical continuity. As Karsten Harries said, "... buildings that deserve to be called works of architecture... do indeed represent ... other buildings that tradition has endowed with a special aura, perhaps because they are associated with a more original and presumably more genuine dwelling. Representing such buildings, works of architecture at the same time represent themselves, drawing from the aura of the represented buildings a special significance for themselves."[2]

Most of these secluded enclaves — symbols of excessive affluence — are designed for the rich. They offer high standards of luxury for those who can afford it. The best of these building types possess levels of sophiscation and quality that other trite hotels clearly lack. Materials are used in a manner which delights while the spaces created are a pleasure to experience. These beautiful resorts, together with houses for the rich, because of their manifestations of a unique life-style, have always serve as models in a 'filtering down' effect. They are an important source of inspiration for many subsequent local works.

The moment such exquisite works are perceived as constituting a particular style, they possess a symbolic ability to create an illusory transcendence of class. Touted as being "authentic", these consumable styles entered the popular imagination as "the real thing", assuming a forceful validity of their own. In the words of George Orwell in his book *1984* : "Who controls the past controls the future. Who controls the present controls the past."

In an incisive essay, Hassan-Uddin Khan wrote: "Constructing buildings using the same materials, the same colours, the same vocabularies ... but with everything obviously more sophiscated, polished, shinier, and so on, means that historical information so absorbed it assumes the aspect of reincarnation."[3] He goes on to question the relationship between this architectural expression and the "real thing — the vernacular born of the tradition of a hundred years. Or is this the real thing?"

These buildings are definitely improved versions of the vernacular, at least at the perceptual level. Umberto Eco echoes this issue when writing about the Palace of Living Arts in Los Angeles. He describes its philosophy as not "We are giving you the reproduction so you will want the original" but rather "We are giving you the reproduction so that you will no longer feel any need for the original."[4] The reproduction always conditions the perceptions of the original, to the extent that the former can even replace the latter to become "the real thing".

But does not such representation of surface forms belong to the realm of applied historicism? The relationships of form, meaning and production have been irrevocably severed. In their rush to embrace a new aesthetic for corporate capitalism, architects have isolated form from meaning. Meaning has been both "transformed" and "transposed". Tafuri calls the former : "the insertion of a theme deeply rooted in a particular, totally different context," and the latter a "definite symbolic charge in asymbolic contexts."[5] Although the aim is to recreate meaning through the use of pre-existing elements, the relationship of the form to its production has also been ruptured. Perez-Gomez has observed that "architects often work under the absurd assumption that meaning and symbol are merely products of the mind, that they can be manufactured *a priori* and that they possess somehow the certainty of number."[6]

Architecture that offers such instant identity has been termed the "communicative sign" by Kenneth Frampton. It "seeks to evoke not a critical perception of reality, but rather the sublimation of a desire for direct experience through the provision of information. Its tactical aim is to attain as economically as possible, a preconceived level of gratification in behavioristic terms."[7] Authenticity certainly cannot be sought in the self-conscious application of such signs. Such historicism can be avoided if the design is based on the generating principles of the past rather than on acknowledged symbols. The generation of similar forms or hybrid versions of them can only result in the stagnation of the operational idea of tradition.

Meaningful directions in contemporary architecture in Southeast Asia can only evolve if there is a deeper understanding and protracted re-evaluation of indigenous building traditions in an ever-expanding field of possibilities than is practised at the moment. The famous quotation from French historian Paul Ricoeur remains unanswered: "There is the paradox: how to become modern and to return to sources, how to revive an old, dormant civilisation and take part in universal civilisation..."

Notes

1   Avis Berman, "The Unflinching Eye of Berenice Abbot", *ART news*, January 1981, pp. 87-88.

2   Karsten Harries, "Representation and Re-Presentation in Architecture", *VIA*, No. 9, The Graduate School of Fine Arts, University of Pennsylvania, 1988, pp. 18.

3   Hassan-Uddin Khan, "Houses: A Synthesis of Tradition and Modernity", *MIMAR: Architecture in Development*, No. 39, June 1991, Concept Media Pte Ltd., pp. 28.

4   Umberto Eco, *Travels in Hyper-Reality*, Picador, 1987, pp. 3-58.

5   Manfredo Tafuri, *Theories and History of Architecture,* Harper & Row, New York, 1976, pp. 110.

6   Alberto Perez-Gomez, *Architecture and the Crisis of Modern Science,* The MIT Press, Cambridge, MA, 1983, pp. 12.

7   Kenneth Frampton, "Towards a Critical Regionalism" in Hal Foster, ed., *The Anti-Aesthetic: Essays on Postmodern Culture*, Bay Press, Port Townsend, Washington, 1983, pp. 126.

Bachelard, Gaston
The Poetics of Space
Beacon Press, Boston, 1963

Bardi, P. M.
The Tropical Gardens of Burle Marx
The Architectural Press, London, 1964

Bussagli, Mario
Oriental Architecture
Rizzoli International Publications, New York,
1989

Chandler, David P., and Steinberg, David Joel
In Search of Southeast Asia — A Modern History
University of Hawaii Press, 1987

Covarrubias, Miguel
Island of Bali
Oxford University Press, Singapore, 1987 (1937)

Dumarcay, Jacques
The House in Southeast Asia
Oxford University Press, Singapore, 1987

Fairservis, Walter A.
Asia — Traditions and Treasures
Harry N. Abrams, Inc., New York, 1981

Fry, Maxwell and Drew, Jane
Tropical Architecture in the Dry and Humid Zones
Robert E Kriegar Publishing Co., Florida, 1982

Hall, Daniel G.
A History of Southeast Asia
Macmillan Education Ltd., London, 1985

Jumsai, Sumet
*Naga — Cultural Origins in Siam and the West
Pacific*
Oxford University Press, New York, 1988

McPhee, Colin
A House in Bali
Oxford University Press, Singapore, 1986

Moholy-Nagy, Sibyl
Native Genius in Anonymous Architecture
Horizon Press, New York, 1957

Moore, Charles W., Mitchell, William J.,
Turnbull, William
The Poetics of Gardens
The MIT Press, Massachusetts, 1988

Osborne, Milton E.
Southeast Asia — An Introductory History
George Allen and Unwin Austria Pte Ltd, 1979

Pickell, David (ed.)
Bali, Islands of the Gods
Periplus Editions, Berkeley, 1990

Powell, Robert
Innovative Architecture of Singapore
Select Books, Singapore, 1989
The Asian House
Select Books, Singapore, 1992

Ramseyer, Urs
The Art and Culture of Bali
Oxford University Press, Oxford, 1977

Rawson, Philip
The Art of Southeast Asia
Thames and Hudson, London, 1967

Ricoeur, Paul
"Universal Civilisation and National Cultures"
in *History and Truth*
Northwestern University Press, Evanston, 1965

Savage, Victor R.
*Western Impressions of Nature and Landscape in
Southeast Asia*
Singapore University Press, Singapore, 1984

Tan, Hock Beng
"Mystical Amandari" in *IQ-Interiors Quarterly,*
Sep-Nov 1990, p. 41-46.
"Coconut Paradise" in *IQ-Interiors Quarterly,*
Sep-Nov 1990, p. 52-54.

"Precima House" in *IQ-Interiors Quarterly,*
Sep-Nov 1990, p. 56-60.
"Eu House" in *IQ-Interiors Quarterly,*
Sep-Nov 1990, p. 62-64.
Shusse Publishing (SEA) Pte Ltd,
Singapore, 1990

Taylor, Brian B. (ed)
Mimar Houses
Concept Media, Singapore, 1987

Warren, William
Thai Style
Times Editions, Singapore, 1988
The Tropical Garden
Thames and Hudson, London, 1991

Waterson, Roxana
*The Living House: An Anthropology of
Architecture in Southeast Asia*
Oxford University Press, Singapore, 1990

White, Stephen
John Thompson: A Window to the Orient
Thames and Hudson, New York, 1986

Yeang, Ken
*Tropical Urban Regionalism — Building in a
South-East Asian City*
Concept Media, Singapore, 1987

Photo Credits

Acknowledgements

The making of "Tropical Architecture and Interiors" has been a long venture that was thoroughly exhausting yet always absorbing. This book would not have been possible without the kind co-operation and generous assistance of a great many people.

In recognition of the help that has been rendered to me, my warmest thanks and acknowledgments to the following: Mark Tan, who was responsible for the embryonic notion of the book, as well as holding the project together through all the difficult stages. Thanks to my wife, Maria, for her invaluable encouragement, for preparing unsurpassed ink drawings in the book and for always been there. In addition I am indebted to Henry Yap for painstakingly reviewing and editing the manuscript.

I also recognise with sincere thanks the contributions of the book designers Molly Sung and Ko Hui Huy of Duet Design. My appreciation for their enthusiasm, openess to ideas and marvellous layouts. Heartfelt thanks to Vivien Wan and my sisiter Hock Suan for typing the manuscript. Special thanks also to Chan Sui Him for his wonderful support, Jimmy C S Lim, Peter Muller, Trina Dingler Ebert, Jean-Noel Guilhem, Shusse Publishing as well as Metropolitan Publishing. Muller has greatly enlightened me on the background to the design approach of his beguiling work of poetry at Amandari.

I also owe grateful appreciation to many others, and I thank you all: Bill Bensley, Mathar Bunnag, Ernesto Bedmar, Kathy Landis, Sonny Chan, Juan Peck Foon, Kong Shee Chong, Leonard Lueras, Low Boon Liang, Robert Powell, Pisit Rojanavanich, Tan Teck Khiam, Agus Wawo-Runtu, Myra A. Wawo-Runtu, Wee Chwee Heng, Michael White, Timothy Evans, Hilary Peralta, Michael Oh, Sunshine Wong, Anthony Lark, Chris Teo, Planteblat Jeff, Mustapha El Kotni, David Good, Oliver Petit, Leslie Loh, Martial Turel, Pamelia Lee, Peggy Fong, Yap Guat Hoon, Thio Lay Hoon, Eddy Koh, Caroline De Lange, Wendy Todd Buchanan, and the late Peter Keys. For early encouragement in my writing and photography, as well as for copy-editing the manuscript, special thanks to Sheila Cheong.

Most significantly, I take great pleasure in thanking all those designers, architects and owners of the buildings illustrated in this book. Their buildings have provided so much wonderful subject matter.

Last, but not least, it is also essential to acknowledge with regret the many more exciting works that cannot be included due to space limitation.

21:29